BRIDPORT PAST

The programme for Bridport's Royal Charter Pageant (24–27 June 1953) when the town celebrated the 700th anniversary of the granting of the charter to the town by Henry III. Princess Margaret was guest of honour.

BRIDPORT PAST

Gerald Gosling

Phillimore

1999

Published by
PHILLIMORE & CO. LTD.
Shopwyke Manor Barn, Chichester, West Sussex

ISBN 1 86077 107 6

Printed and bound in Great Britain by
BIDDLES LTD.
Guildford, Surrey

Contents

List of Illustrations

Frontispiece: Bridport's Royal Charter Pageant programme

Acknowledgements

Hilary Giles, who so kindly allowed me access to the Hounsell family album and thus to most of the pictures in this book.

Jack Thomas of Uplyme, who read the script and made several sensible suggestions. Any subsequent errors are because I did not listen to all of them. Keith Alner, who read my script with the eyes of a local historian. Both Jack and Keith Fountaine of Axminster were more than helpful with some photographic work.

Bridport Town Council and the Town Clerk, Roger Davies, who so kindly allowed me to take pictures of the inside of the Town Hall and make copies of some of their pictures.

Anita Travers of the Kingstone Historic Buildings Consultants of Exeter, who kindly allowed me to make use of her research notes on Bridport Town Hall.

Bill Croad, Gerald Marsh, Pamela Puley and Marjorie Randall, who took the time and trouble to talk to me about the Bridport of their youth.

Research has been necessary at both Bridport Library and the Dorset Record Office at Dorchester, especially the library where the staff have been even more courteous and helpful than duty requires them to be, especially when I inadvertently took a key away with me.

The Bridport News, who have faithfully recorded Bridport's past since 1855, have been more than helpful, particularly Rosemary Lewis.

Jenny Rockett, the Hospital Manager's Secretary, and Bridport Community Hospital for permission to reproduce part of the 'Great Map of Bridport'. Reverend Maureen Allchin for kind permission to reproduce the photograph of Major Farrer's memorial at St Mary's and David Lawrence of Edwards Sports Products Ltd.

The following have kindly allowed me to reproduce photographs: Mary Bailey, 52; Donald Balson, 35, 121; Les Berry, 109, 138; Bridport Community Hospital, 19; Bridport Town Council, 1, 144-47; Ray and Frances Buzza, 34, 141; Maureen Allchin, 140; Sir John Colfox, 60; David Lawrence of Edwards Sports Products, 102, 107; Keith Fountaine, 33, 76; Hilary Giles, 2, 5-8, 10, 11, 13, 17, 18, 20, 21, 26-32, 36-41, 43-47, 51, 56, 59, 63, 64, 69-72, 75, 77, 79-84, 86-98, 100, 101, 104, 105, 111, 112, 114, 116, 117, 119, 120, 122-25, 127-35, 137-39, 143, 149; Pamela Puley, frontispiece, 3, 4, 9, 12, 16, 22, 25, 42, 48, 49, 53-55, 61, 62, 65-67, 68, 73, 74, 78, 85, 110, 113, 126, 142, 143, 148; Marjorie Randall, 23, 24, 50, 57, 58; Jim Rowe, 115; Brian Stidwell, 118; Ken Symes, 14, 15, 99, 103, 106, 136; and Jack Thomas, 108.

Chapter One

Beginnings

A clean, sweet-smelling town where, I should not be surprised to learn, all the Christian virtues arise and where, certainly, the inhabitants, one and all, have the whimsical air of mildly interested spectators in the drama of human life ... an unmistakable air of benevolence, even in the tradesmen, who absurdly keep their shops open for altruistic principles and for the convenience of purchasers, rather than for any base dealings and the making of a profit.

Charles Harper, Dorset Coast, *1905.*

The origins of the place-names of many towns and villages are shrouded in the mists of history. Others—Axminster and Charmouth are two local examples—point an incontrovertible finger to their beginnings. Bridport is closer to the second category although mild arguments were once raised as to its actual meaning. Bridport, the port on the Brid (Bredy), seems obvious enough, but 'port' may not have had the meaning we give to the word today; rather, it was a place with a market. Hutchins, writing in 1774, certainly thought so. 'This town', he said, 'takes its name from the river Birt or Brit', and he dismisses, quite rightly, other suggestions, including that of Bruteport, where Brute was said to have landed. Thomas Hardy, at least, agreed with Hutchins when he called it Port Bredy, the setting for his *Fellow Travellers* novel. And he stayed with the name in *The Mayor of Casterbridge*.

Dr. Rendall Harris once advanced the theory that there was an early Egyptian occupation of southern Britain, pointing out that Eype Mouth and the frequently found West Dorset family name of Guppy are derived from WP or VP, the sign of the Egyptian god Osiris. Be that as it may (or may not)!

There is no evidence of Roman activity as such in Bridport, although their great road from Dorchester to Exeter passed just to the north and may even have been what became the modern A35 as it left the extreme western part of the town. The Saxons would have reached Bridport, even if they did not colonise it at once, at the beginning of the seventh century; in 610 they won the decisive battle of Beandun (said to be Bindon just over the border in Devon above Axmouth) and began their occupation of Devonshire. Tradition, if not fact, gives Blood Lane, sometimes Dead Man's Lane, as a place on Bothen Wood Hill where a river of blood flowed after a battle between the Saxons and the Danes. When this was is unclear; perhaps in 833 when, according to Hutchins again, 35 ships attacked Charmouth and its neighbourhood. But, sadly, most of Bridport's Saxon story lies hidden and is likely to remain so.

We do know that the town was one of four in Dorset with a mint in Saxon times, the other three being Shaftesbury, Dorchester and

1 The Mayor's chair at the Town Hall in front of the board listing his predecessors and their years in office.

2 In all probability this portion of Lyme Road (now West Road), seen behind the old pond, was part of the Roman Dorchester-Exeter road. The pond, once part of a mill stream, has long since been filled in. Today Blackburn's foundry is just out of sight on the right. A foundry is known to have existed on the site as far back as the mid-18th century.

Wareham, and that the finding of Dorset coins in Scandinavia suggests that the Vikings had been active in the area.

It is probable that the first Bridport did not extend as far north as today's East Street-West Street axis but was centred around St Mary's Church in South Street. The northern part of the town became established after Domesday Book was written. Joseph Maskell, writing in 1855, casts some doubt on this, questioning whether St Mary's Church had existed on its present site prior to its building (or rebuilding) at the end of the 14th century. He says,

> it is quite possible that there may have been a church in Bridport, upon the site of St Mary's before this time. In my opinion, however, the first parish church did not stand upon the present site, but in another part of the town.

He reckons this to have been the Town Hall, in which case our centring of Saxon Bridport on St Mary's would be incorrect. Few, if any, modern authorities would agree with him, however, even if Leland, over four centuries ago, said of the junctions of East, West and South Streets that is was 'wher sum say that the paroch chirch was yn old tyme'. The combination of a wide market street and the still-evident burgage plots on both its sides still suggest South Street.

The *Castle Inn*, which became the Oddfellows' Hall, then the Conservative Club and later, in 1932, as a gift of a Captain Codd, the Bridport Museum, is said to have got its name from the old (Saxon) castle that once stood there. It is more or less where the entrance to the old Saxon town would have been, an obvious spot for fortifications, and there is a reference to a messuage being sold in South Street 'without the Bars' and on 'the north side of the land which was formerly Stephen Alymund's'. There are later references to both 'Castleheigh' (a bequest of 1390) and 'Castlehay' (also wills).

3 The Castle, South Street, at the turn of the century when it was the Conservative Club. Thought once to have been the home of a chantry priest, it stands on the supposed site of a Saxon castle. If so, it is appropriate that, since 1932, it has been the home of Bridport Museum.

According to K.J. Penn, in his *Historical Towns in Dorset*, Henry Plantagenet (later Henry II), during his mother Matilda's struggles with Stephen, 'boldly took by storm the town called Bridport and the castellan of the place who had made submission to the King [Stephen]'. As a castellan was a governor of a castle it is fairly safe to assume that there was a castle or fortification in the town; whether in South Street or Castle Square, which is half a mile or so to the south and behind the Chantry, is open to question. The present 'Castle' is an attractive building in Ham stone with a quaint room above the porch and handsome stone mullions to its windows. It was seriously damaged by an 1876 fire but restored carefully enough not to leave any scars.

4   Bridport Borough coat of arms.

Claims to Bridport's castle are also advanced on the Corporation shield, which includes a castle standing on wavy blue lines in its design. What seems to be a portcullis in the entrance to the castle is actually spinning cogs, a reference to the town's main industry.

We are on firmer ground with Domesday Book, which states that there were 120 houses at Bridport in the time of Edward the Confessor (1042-1066); this suggests a population of around 500. Domesday goes on to tell us that the town was 'responsible for all the services to the King and paid land tax for 5 hides [300-500 acres] of land', that is to say, half a mark of silver to the use of the house servants of the King exclusive of the customary dues which belong to the farm of one night. 'In that place there was one moneyer who rendered to the King one mark of silver and 20 shillings when the money was changed.' Bridport had obviously fallen on harder times in the aftermath of the Conquest; Domesday Book, which was compiled in 1086, goes on to say 'Now there are in that place 100 houses and 20 are so dilapidated those who remain in them cannot pay the land tax.'

The reference to dues which belong to the farm of one night meant that Bridport had an obligation to provide hospitality to the king for the period stated. We know John took up the offer on two occasions in 1201 and 1204, when he came west to hunt at Powerstock Forest, a little to the north of the town.

Not all that long afterwards, on 22 June 1253, John's son Henry III (1216-72) granted the town its first charter, which was reaffirmed during Henry VIII's reign (1509-47). Henry III's charter is among many valuable documents in the Borough Archives and it states that Bridport should

thenceforward be a free borough and that the men and their heirs for ever should hold the borough with the liberties and customs to the same borough appertaining at the yearly rent they had before paid to the King and 40 shillings yearly in addition.

On view inside the Town Hall is a list of the bailiffs from 1290 to 1834, and among the records stored in that building is the original Precept from the Sheriff of Dorset to the Bailiff of the Town calling for the election of two Members of Parliament. The right to return two Members was granted by Edward I and Bridport continued to do so even after the 1832 Reform Act, which reduced its West Dorset neighbour Lyme Regis's Westminster representation from two to one. In 1868, however, Bridport's number of M.P.s was also reduced to one. Further parliamentary reform in 1885 placed it in the West Dorset constituency in which it still remains.

The two bailiffs were elected from the 12 burgesses who had been empowered by the grant of 1253; the number was increased to 15 by James I. The original right of election of the M.P.s was 'in the inhabitants at large, being housekeepers or potwallers' (anyone who boils a pot there, i.e. has a house in which he lives and cooks), says Hutchins. The first two men to be called to Westminster by Edward I

5 Although the milk float indicates that the age of the horse was not yet past, the horseless carriages were already taking over, with the Lyme Regis bus lumbering into West Allington in the early 1920s.

6 The *Plymouth Inn*, West Allington, *c*.1907. It advertised good stables at the time.

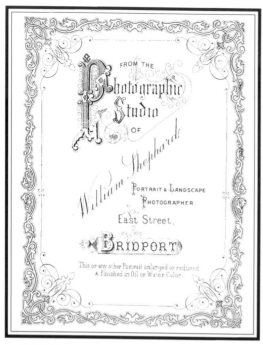

7 William Shephard photographed much of turn-of-the-century Bridport and its inhabitants from his East Street studio, and is responsible for many of the pictures in this book.

8 Bradpole's West Dorset Historical Pageant was always lavishly costumed, never more so than here in July 1911 when Queen Elizabeth I's escort was on parade.

to sit in the Model Parliament were Thomas Newburgh and Robert Hill in 1295.

Henry's charter was confirmed by subsequent monarchs, including Elizabeth I (1558-1603), who also granted the town the right to hold three annual fairs and a Saturday market. She obviously appreciated the value of Bridport to herself and to the realm which depended largely on the town's manufacturing base for the ropes and sails for both the navy and the many adventurers-cum-pirates, some from just along the coast in Devonshire. This had been especially true at the time of the Armada, when the threat of invasion by the Spaniards was very real. Dorset in general, and Bridport in particular, feared for the safety of the area in the event of a successful forcing of the Channel by the Armada in 1588. In May of that year the Dorset forces amounted to some 3,000 men, most of them centred in

Dorchester but there were small detachments at both Bridport and Lyme Regis. The Armada sailed and was harried up the Channel by Lord Howard's fleet, running battles being fought as it made its majestic path across Lyme Bay. According to the celebrated historian, Arthur Bryant, in his *The Elizabethan Deliverance,* a continuous stream of small boats poured out of the little Dorset ports of Lyme, Charmouth and Bridport bringing the English Fleet volunteers, supplies of fresh food, fresh vegetables and ammunition, as fast as the shore authorities could requisition them, while spectators, peering anxiously seawards through the summer haze, crowded the low hills above Chesil Beach and West Bay.

I am sure that people did crowd to watch, or listen, to the running battle, but whether the English ships would have been in need of fresh food and vegetables so soon after leaving

9 Panoramic Bridport in 1903. Much of the green-field area on the right has vanished beneath the sprawl of post-war development. Plainly seen here is St Swithin's in the middle and, on the left, North Mills, now an industrial estate.

10 Henry Hounsell, Mayor of Bridport, 1939-40. The Mayor's chain consists of monograms and shields linked with ornate initial 'B's. The shields bear the names of the bailiffs. A gold clasp has 'JCP' in red enamel and is engraved with 'given by J.C. Palmer' on the reverse. Various monograms are engraved, such as the central one which has 'WJ' after William James, Mayor in 1897. The Mayor's badge has the inscription 'Bryde-porte, incorporated 1237, Henry III'. It is surmounted with the arms of the Borough and has the arms of England on the left and those of the United Kingdom on the right. There is a small enamel picture of the Town Hall borne in oak leaves at the base.

Plymouth is open to question. Still, it is good to think that some Bridport men may have been ferried out to help Lord Howard and Sir Francis Drake in their fight with the enemy, and that when they boarded the ships, they actually clambered up rope ladders made in their home town.

In around 1540, the celebrated itinerist Leland had visited the town and he tells us:

From Chidwik to Britport, by corne, pasure and wood, two miles. At the west ende of the town rennith a river, and going a mile lower enterith the ocean. Nature has so set this ryver mouth in a valley betweixt two hilles, that with cost the se might brought in, and ther an haven made. Britport, of some written Bruteport, is a fair larg town, and the cheif streat ot lyith in length from West to Est; ther crosse another fair strete in middle of it, into the South. At the North end of this streate is a chapelle of St Andrea's, wher sum say that the paroch chirch was yn old tyme. The paroch chirch of the town is now standing in the South end of this streate. Ther was in sight or ever I cam over the ryver into Britport a lazier house, and not far off a chapelle of St Magdalene, in which is a centaur founded; and over the bridge a little by West in the town, is a chapelle of St John; The town longish to the king, and has privileges for a market and two bailiffs. At Bridporth be made good daggers.

Leland was at fault here. Bridport did not make daggers, good or bad. But he had heard of a 'Bridport dagger', the criminal's slang term for the rope made in the town and used by the hangman to despatch his customers, and obviously thought it was a reference to a real dagger.

The grant of Charles I included the right to be a Court of Record and, from 1625 until 1825, Bridport, along with Sherborne, Blandford and Shaftesbury, was the site of Dorset's Quarter Sessions once a year.

Little is known about the suffering of Bridport during the Black Death but it would have been among its earliest victims, the plague making its first appearance in England in 1348 just a few miles along the coast at the port of Melcombe Regis, which is now united with Weymouth. The disease was almost certainly bubonic plague and was spread by the bites of rat-borne fleas. Perhaps the best indication of the extent to which the Black Death affected the town is the number of wills made there at the time. As only the rich made them, one will per year was a reasonable average in a town like Bridport. In 1348 as many as 18 were known in the town. In 1665, on the other hand, we know that the Great Plague killed so many people that, in the near-empty town, 'the grass grew in the streets'. Things

11   Victoria Grove seen on a postcard sent to Miss Alice Hounsell of Laurel House in North Allington in 1905. The message includes, 'Here is a view you would always have, but for No. 14 obstructing it'. So, one can only presume that the photographer was standing in No. 14's garden in North Allington when he took it.

12   Beach & Co. in East Street was once the *George*, the inn at which Charles II stopped on his way to Dorchester after failing to secure a passage to France from Charmouth. Their speciality was Dr. Roberts' Poor Man's Friend Ointment which was said to remove 'all unsightly blotches, Pimples and Chilblains' among other things.

came to such a sorry state that an order was made at Dorset's Easter Sessions that a collection of £40 be made each week in the divisions of Sherborne, Dorchester and Bridport. The money was to be used to bring sustenance and relief to the people of the Borough of Bridport. The reference to 'a near-empty town' might not be an exaggeration; the parish register records 80 deaths between August and November and in that winter whole families were wiped out.

Disease of a different kind reached Bridport in 1757, when over fifty inhabitants died from smallpox. The disease remained a killer on and off until the mid-19th century when the vaccination of infants was made compulsory.

Dorset was largely for Parliament during the Civil War, Bridport's main action being on account of its proximity to Lyme Regis, which was besieged by the Royalists. A Lieutenant Lea garrisoned Bridport on 10 June 1643.

In 1651, when the town was full of Parliamentarian foot soldiers preparing for an expedition to Jersey, Charles II came west seeking passage to France after his defeat at the Battle of Worcester. Arrangements were made for a Lyme Regis master called Stephen Limber, who was about to make a trip to St Malo, to take him across the Channel for £60. Limber was told that he was helping a couple to elope, that they were staying at the *Queen's Arms* in Charmouth and that he was to pick them up from Charmouth beach. But his wife had heard a proclamation at Lyme Fair that same morning warning of the severe penalties to be forfeit by anyone helping Charles Stuart. It made her suspicious about his intention to put to sea before he had loaded his cargo and she locked him in his bedroom after, we are told, first hiding his trousers. When no boat arrived at Charmouth, Charles and his party decided to make for Bridport, though not before they had aroused the suspicions of the local blacksmith who had shoed the horse of Lord Wilt, one of

Charles's companions, who declared that the horse had previously been shoed in three counties 'and that one of them was Worcester'. The blacksmith told Bartholomew Wesley, the local minister, of his suspicions and the militia were alerted.

Meanwhile the King had arrived in Bridport where he brazenly pushed his way through the soldiers in the yard at the *George*, waiting there for the best part of an hour before food was forthcoming. Here, again, an ostler thought he knew Charles's face but was told that he was probably from Exeter, the ostler's home town, where he (Charles) had worked as a boy. The man may have accepted this, but it was obviously time to move on, the royal party heading along the London road towards Dorchester, in which direction it was soon followed by the militia under Captain Macey. Some sixth sense caused Charles to alter course and make instead for Trent Manor near Yeovil, where he had stayed before journeying to Charmouth. He took a small lane just outside Bridport and, after a night at an inn in Broadwindsor, made good his escape back to Trent and, eventually, to Shoreham in Sussex from where he successfully crossed to France.

In 1901, the 250th anniversary of the escape, a block of Bothenhampton stone was placed at the entrance to Lea Lane recording that Charles had turned there and avoided capture. At the same time a commemorative pilgrimage was made by motor cars following the route the King took from Worcester to Bridport. During their stay in the Bridport area the party was entertained to lunch at Catherston Hall by Colonel Bullen.

Charles's illegitimate son by Lucy Walters, the ill-fated Duke of Monmouth, was responsible for the next military disturbance in the town, soon after he landed at Lyme Regis in 1685. He sent Lord Grey with 300 men from that little port in an overnight march on Bridport to attack the Dorset militia which was quartered there. A dawn attack on Sunday met with little resistance, despite Lord Grey's men

13 & 14 *Above and right.* Two contrasting views of South Street. The first, dated 1868, is looking away from the Town Hall with the *Cross Keys* on the immediate left. Right, some forty years later there seems more life around and both sides of the street have gained some trees.

15 *Above right.* South Street around 1913 with one of the town's earliest motor cars parked casually by the pavement.

being outnumbered, the militia rapidly with-
drawing to the eastern end of the town after
they had been fired on. There they were forced
by their officers to make a stand. In the centre
of the town, shots had been exchanged after
someone fired out of one of the *Bull*'s upstairs
windows at the 40 members of Lord Grey's
horse which had been brought up by Colonel
Venner. The inn was stormed and two of
its defenders were killed, one by Colonel
Venner who was himself then hit in the
stomach. Monmouth's men then returned their
attentions to the militia who were guarding
the bridge at the end of East Street but, when
their fire was returned and two of their number
were killed, they quickly withdrew, leaving a
rearguard at the West Street bridge to exchange
insults (but not shots) with the militia.

Soon after the retreat to Lyme Regis,
Monmouth led his motley army out of that
town towards Axminster where he turned
north-east for Taunton, Sedgmoor and, eventually, the block on Tower Hill. He was
probably wise to leave Dorset when he did.
Two days later, Lord Churchill, the future
illustrious Duke of Marlborough, led two troops
of dragoons and four troops of Lord Oxford's
Regiment of Horse through Bridport in hot
pursuit of Monmouth's army, mostly of
peasants. Churchill's ancestors came from
Dorset, and he himself was born at Ashe House,
between Axminster and Musbury, a few miles
over the border in Devonshire. When the
infamous Judge Jeffreys came westwards to
distribute King James's vengeance, John Sprake,
Benjamin Sandford and John Bennett (from
Lyme Regis) and nine others were hanged,
drawn and quartered in the town.

Christopher Bettiscombe from Vere's
Farm, now Vearse Farm, just to the west of
Bridport, had also been 'out with Monmouth'
and was later tried and condemned to death at
Dorchester after he turned down an offer of
clemency from Judge Jeffreys if he would
impeach other rebels. The sentence was carried
out at Lyme Regis, and Bettiscombe, taken by

cart to his death, is said to have looked at his
'fair home' as he passed by and claimed that he
was on his way to a 'fairer home'.

The Bettiscombe family, who were still
living at Vearse in the early years of the 20th
century, were only the third family to occupy
the farm in nine centuries, Vearse being held
by the de Vere family, hence its original name,
from the Conquest to the time of Henry III.
A Bridport merchant called Mountford then
held it for a short time before it passed into the
hands of the Bettiscombes.

Bridport recovered from all the alarms of
the 17th century and prospered. This prosperity
brought a new town hall, courtesy of an Act of
Parliament of 1785 (24 Geo III c.xci) passed for

> taking down the Market House and rebuilding
> the same, together with a Session or Court
> House, in a more convenient situation; for
> the removing of the Shambles or Butcher
> Row; for better paving, cleansing, lighting,
> and watching the said Borough; for removing
> and preventing Nuisances and Annoyances;
> and for prohibiting the covering of any new
> Houses or Buildings, within the said Borough,
> with Thatch.

Thus the council was able to get rid of the
mouldering remains of the old, long-since
disused St Andrew's chapel and at the same
time remove the old shambles which ran down
one side of the road, obstructing the free passage
of traffic, a definite hazard to the health and
cleanliness of the town. An important by-
product of the act saw the reduction of the
amount of thatch in the town in future years,
a wise move that saved Bridport some of the
disastrous fires endured by many of its neighbours.

The new building, the work of the
architect William Tyler, R.A., was an impos-
ing centrepiece, one which it is easily possible
to imagine inspiring the pride of local inhabitants whenever they passed it. And why not?
Not only was Bridport's trade connection with
the Baltic evident in the specifications sent out
to contractors who wished to submit tenders

16 The Council Chamber at the Town Hall around 1901, still gas-lit and with a sturdy heating appliance on the right. Happily, for the public's comfort, the old wooden benches are long since gone.

stating that the floor was to be of 'good Riga or Memel timber', but also, throughout the considerable detail in the specifications quality was always much in evidence. Reference is made to 'best Portland Stone', 'good sound brick, proper beams, Deal board, strong lintels and ridge hips, and gutters covered with lead of 7lb to the foot'. It was meant to last, and it has, even if there was talk in the 1960s of knocking it down and replacing it with a roundabout.

Mention is made of a 'clock in the Tympanum of the Pediment if necessary', but apparently it was not thought so, the present cupola and clock being added in 1804 as a gift of Sir Evan Nepean, one of Bridport's M.P.s between 1802-7. It stayed there until 1919 when the dials were replaced and the works sold. Twelve years later, in 1931, three new striking bells were installed, bringing complaints

about their noise during the night. Similar complaints were made immediately after the Second World War, when the National Fire Service wanted to continue using the air-raid siren on the Town Hall as a fire alarm. In the face of considerable opposition the fire service won but had to agree to the siren only being used between 8 a.m. and 6 p.m. The complaints were aired at a Town Council meeting at which Councillor D.H. Rhys headed the opposition by saying, 'Surely we are not going to perpetuate the horrible howling of Weary Willie in this town?' He was told it was the All Clear that would be sounded and not the actual air-raid warning. No one thought to ask him what his sentiments would have been if his house had burnt down because there was no other quick way to alert the firemen.

The old building and shambles were demolished in February 1786, the five (main)

17 & 18 At work and play in Edwardian Bridport. Above, the Hounsell family relax over the tea cups at the back of their home in Laurel House, North Allington. To the right, they get stuck into the spring cleaning.

contractors who began work on the new Town Hall being David Fudge, responsible for the bricklaying, plastering and tiling at £670; James Hamilton, of Melcombe Regis, the Portland stone work (£400); John Conway, William Bearn and Abraham Selwood, carpentry and joining (£626), and Abraham Selwood, the lead work (£99).

The finished building contained a ground-floor market with no fewer than 37 butcher's stalls. On the upper floor was the Council Chamber which was also to serve as a magistrates' court. Originally a schoolroom had been envisaged but it was left out because of the cost.

The Town Hall has stared out over the inexorable passing of Bridport's days for just over two centuries, much of the time as the centre of the town's life; it was here that important announcements were once made and, after their crying, were nailed outside in notice form. Although a menace to modern-day traffic, its only moment of real danger came during an air raid in the Second World War when nearby bombs caused death and damage, a little of it to the Town Hall.

Bridport's prosperity was given a fresh lease of life by the increase in the Royal Navy's demands for ropes and cordage during the French Wars at the end of the 18th century. That prosperity is reflected in the town's having as many as three surgeons, William Carpenter, Simon Robinson and Samual Dunne, which was a high figure for a town of its size when the poor could hardly afford such luxuries. Looking after Bridport's legal interests were three attorneys, Edward Dally, John Symes and John Tomlyns. It was a self-sufficient town. Between the two rivers that cross the ends of West Street and East Street, and down South Street as far as, say, St Mary's

Church, each and every one of more than 3,000 inhabitants could get all that was needed to sustain whatever standard of living they were accustomed to. There were at least nine grocers, a victualler, a confectioner, three cutlers, as many bakers, two millers (almost certainly there were others just outside the parish boundaries), a hatter, two tailors, a collar maker, two hairdressers, a bookseller, two coopers, six maltsters, a currier, a silversmith, a post maker, and, not unnaturally for a town with a harbour, there were cordwainers, a sailcloth maker, a ship builder and a tide watcher. The latter was actually a customs officer who 'waited for the ships to come in on one or other of the two daily tides and checked their cargoes for dutiable goods'. There was also Frank King, 'a slop-man', whose job was the removal of night-waste.

Such a prosperous town was able to celebrate national days of rejoicing in style. For the Coronation of George III and Queen Charlotte a huge bonfire was lit to the south of the town and the bailiffs and burgesses invited

19 The Great Map of Bridport. Started in autumn 1992, the magnificent embroidered map of the town, which is hanging in the town's hospital, was made by over 200 people, contains over 300 individual pieces and has more than two million stitches. The piece seen here contains the Town Hall (right rear) and parts of South and West Streets.

20   The proclamation of King George V outside the front of the Town Hall on 11 May 1910.

43 of the principal gentlemen of the town to attend, suggesting that they meet them at the Guildhall and, after walking to the fire, to return there and join them in more celebrations.

It was much the same later in George's reign when, on Thursday 14 July 1814, a Festival of Peace was held in the town to mark what the locals thought was the end of Napoleon. One hundred days later the festival may have seemed a million years away when the news reached Bridport that the French Emperor had left Elba, but at the time the huge parade through Bridport had nothing but enjoyment on its mind when it formed up in

Chard's Meadow for a nine o'clock start. It must have made an impressive sight as it headed into a town decorated with bunting, flags and greenery, and with four uniformed trumpeters on grey horses leading the way. They were followed by the town's sergeant-at-mace, the churchwardens, the clergy, in gowns, the bailiffs and burgesses, the ladies of the committee and other ladies of Bridport whom they might wish to include, and then a band and two yeomen of cavalry. 'Neptune' and 'Britannia' were seated in a car drawn by four white horses and supported on each side by 12 sailors, followed by another two yeomen of cavalry. A splendid

21 Jam, Jerusalem and a chance to show off the hats for Bridport Women's Institute Choir in 1921.

KNIGHT'S BULL HOTEL, BRIDPORT.

THE ONLY FREE HOTEL IN THE TOWN.

General Posting
and ::
Livery Stables.

Wedding
Carriages.

Funeral Cars.

Pleasure Parties
specially catered
for.

Omnibuses
meet all Trains.

Good Stock
and :
Assembly Rooms.

Horses taken
in to
Livery and Bait.

TELEPHONE No. 0196.
TELEGRAMS—
" BULL HOTEL."

Wine and Spirit Merchant.   G. A. KNIGHT, PROPRIETOR.

22   The *Bull*, East Street, around 1902 when its bus still 'met all trains'.

array of the town's workforce, headed by the foremen of the local warehouses, marched behind. In order, the workers were the combers, spinners, rope and line makers, artificers, etc. from Golding's factory, bleachers and weavers and bag weavers. A second band was followed by a plough which, drawn by four horses and attended by six young rustics in carters' frocks and bearing some implement of husbandry, broke the workers' ranks. Behind the plough followed bakers, carpenters, joiners and cabinet makers, shoe makers, coopers and brewers, tailors three deep, masons, blacksmiths, painters, glaziers, plumbers, collar makers, shipwrights and sail makers. Another break was formed by the town's Sunday School children, and then came butchers, with marrow bones and cleavers. Anyone not included in the official parade but who wanted to march was allowed to bring up the rear.

The parade made its way through the town to West Bridge where it turned on itself and marched back to the Town Hall, turning down South Street as far as the toll-gate. Here it again turned and marched back into Bridport then turned right into East Street and on towards the East Bridge, ending where it had started in Chard's Meadow.

To prevent confusion, each trade had first formed up in private processions and marched to the assembly point where Mr. Marshall and Mr. Templar, the mounted marshals, slotted them into their correct positions in the main parade. The vice-presidents of the tables, decorated with blue cockades and carrying seven-foot deal wands, walked on either side of the procession and kept back the crowds.

Later the town clerk ascended a stage outside the Town Hall and read a proclamation 'in an audible voice, occasionally turning to each street'. This was followed by *God Save The King* and *Rule Britannia* in 'full voice'. After the procession, all those with tickets for the outdoor feast that was held in a now unknown field, but most likely the Fair Field, assembled outside the dwelling house of the vice-president whose name was on the back of their ticket and marched under him to the field and sat at the table with numbers marked on their tickets. Each of the vice-presidents had brought a carving knife and fork and a gravy spoon, and they were also to ensure that their tables had six stewards, four as carriers, two as butlers, and that their tables were kept supplied with food. The food on offer included six dishes of meat, eight dishes of puddings baked by Mr. Samuel Stevens, and six dishes of potatoes boiled at William Colfox's. Each person at the feast had to be clean and decently dressed and had to bring a knife, fork and pint cup.

On a more sombre royal occasion in January 1820, the coffin party taking the late Edward, Duke of Kent, the then infant Queen Victoria's impoverished father, stopped at Bridport on its way back to London after the Duke's death at Sidmouth, where he had gone to escape his creditors. The procession arrived at St Mary's Church between eight and nine in the evening, passing through huge crowds which had gathered, in complete silence, to pay their respects. The coffin stayed the night inside the church with the Bridport Light Horse on watch, their band playing the Dead March from *Saul* when it was placed inside and again in the morning before it left.

Other royal occasions include Joanne of Navarre and her three children being greeted by the prominent townspeople after she landed at West Bay in 1403 on her way to London to meet Henry IV, to whom she was already married by proxy. William IV may not have visited Bridport, but the people recognised a good excuse for celebrating, constructing a crown of coloured lights which was hung outside the Town Hall to mark his coronation, and coronation bread and beer was distributed. The passing through the town of both the Grand Duke Michael of Russia and the Duchess of Clarence (later William IV's Queen Adelaide) is mentioned in the 19th-century diaries of Maria Carter, daughter of Joshua Carter, a local wool stapler; and George III would have passed through on 13 August 1783, the day he journeyed from Weymouth to visit Thomas Whitty's still fairly new carpet factory at Axminster.

Chapter Two

Continuations

It is large, and has a very respectable appearance; the principal streets are broad and spacious, and many of the houses new brick buildings. The inhabitants are mostly engaged in the manufacture of seins and nets of all sorts, lines, twines, small cordage, and sail-cloth

Bath to Bridport coach itinerary, *c*.1818

At the end of the 18th century Bridport was a good town to live in. There was plenty of work and the governing body made sure it kept abreast of the advances that were slowly raising the standards of living throughout the country. Hutchins, in 1774, found that 'a good many brick houses have been built and the streets [are] well paved', a claim underlined by the quotation from an old coaching itinerary printed some forty years later. Joseph Maskell claimed, however, that the buildings, chiefly of stone, were said 'to be rather mean'. There were about 250 of them and Maskell, who was there at the time and is, therefore, a credible witness, tells that there was not a lot of improvement by 1855, when he found Bridport was in need of a better class of cottages and deplored the lack of privacy in those that existed. He said that generally only one bedroom had a door and you had to go through other bedrooms to get to it. It was a problem that still existed in some rural areas as late as the 1950s—my own grandparents' home at Sidmouth being an instance.

UTILITIES

The town, which had the first gasworks in Dorset around 1832, was also the first in the county to have gas street lighting, in 1844, when the Town Hall was lit (outside) with three attractive, three-branched pendants, and the Council Chamber inside by a single, double-branched pendant. After the Crimean War, when it was thought fitting to illuminate the Town Hall clock permanently as a 'Peace Demonstration', gas lighting was used but it proved to be more costly than the estimated £10 per annum. Even so it was not until 1972 that the clock was powered by electricity, at a cost of £450. St Mary's Church in South Street had gas lighting as early as 1838, which must have been a great boon to worshippers who, before the gas arrived, would have attended services in the winter months lit only by stuttering candles.

The Bridport Gas Company moved into their new premises in South Street in 1900, and held a celebratory dinner in the board-room. The building was constructed of local Bothenhampton stone with Ham Hill stone dressing.

References are made to public toilets at least as early as 1880, when a gas light was 'to be put in a urinal near the Market House'. There had also been, in Downe Street, a toilet and public baths which were acquired by the Town Council around 1899. A 'Ladies' arrived

23 William Morey's sale catalogue for the furniture
at Magdala House in West Allington on 2 June 1931.

in 1912 when the sanitary committee, after
listening to complaints about offenders
damaging the public lavatories (at the Town
Hall?), later agreed to provide a public lavatory
for the use of women on the east side of the
Town Hall.

The passage there between the *Greyhound*
and the Town Hall is known as 'Buckydoo'.
Some suggest that it comes from Buck and
Doe, because of the public toilets close at hand,
but few can be certain as to why it is so
called because there is no positive reason for
the name. Many historians refer to the
connection between the local lock-up and the
Spanish word *bocardo*, or gaol. Even if an article
in *The Guardian* in 1913 (reprinted in *The*
Bridport News) supported this, it must be
fanciful. If the word comes down to us from
the mists of time, it is not likely that the
16th-century English dislike of Spain, particularly strong in the West Country, would
tolerate a Spanish name.

COMMERCE

The account books of Morey & Sons, Bridport's
leading auctioneers, who started trading in the
town in the 1860s, have been preserved at the
Dorset Record Office and they allow us a
fascinating look into the town's commerce
during the following forty years or so. Morey
& Sons were primarily repository salesmen
holding their fortnightly sales at the Templar
Hall. But they also did a good trade in livestock at Bridport market and on fair days, when
two or three thousand pounds went through
their books. Under their hammer also went
such items as a cider mill (press?), firewood,
a wagon, a hay cart, cider casks and trefolium
at Hill Farm, Salwayash, as well as six tons of
bagged potatoes (they made £7 2s. 7d.), furniture, cows, horses, pigs and dead or live
poultry.

Nor were they fussy about where they
held a sale, putting up cattle and dairy goods in
a sale at North Mills, and a bay mare in East
Street 'opposite the *Greyhound*'. It made £9,

24 Magdala House was formerly the home of Mr. and Mrs. William Randall, and can be seen here around 1928.

25 Staff at the Milk Factory in East Road, 1933.

out of which Morey & Son took a nine-shilling commission. Mr. John Garland, late of the *Hit and Miss Inn* in South Street, had his furniture sold for £4 1s. 0d. It was bad enough that your life's chattels were disposed of for such a paltry sum; having the sale out in the open opposite a rival ale house, the *Rook* in West Street, was adding insult to insult. Cider at Brightshay Farm fetched £83 4s. 0d. I doubt if it made more than a penny a pint which suggests that around 2,500 gallons changed hands.

The firm, who often used the town crier at a cost of between one and two shillings a cry to announce their more important sales, were once, in 1881, both seller and customer, when they put six fireproof safes under the hammer. Three of the safes were bought by Morey & Son themselves at £3 each.

POLITICS

As mentioned earlier, Bridport's right to send an M.P. to Westminster, reduced from two in 1868, ended in 1885 when it was placed in the West Dorset constituency. Perhaps it was just as well. During the last two elections to be held in the town, Bridport seethed with printed, scurrilous innuendo of the sort that would keep modern-day lawyers in work for years with the ensuing libel actions. The last Bridport-only election took place in 1880 and was conducted against a background of liquid bribery that overturned the 1875 result which had seen the election of the Liberal candidate Pandeli Rali. He had been adopted to succeed Mr. Thomas Mitchell, who had died in office after being returned unopposed in the previous two elections. In 1875 Rali had beaten off Sir Charles Whetham, a poor, and local, Conservative choice as candidate, by 620 to 189 votes.

The Colfox family were staunch Liberals and naturally upset when the 1880 Bridport result went against the national trend which had seen Gladstone's new Liberal government end Disraeli's six-year reign as Prime Minister. Mary Colfox, writing to her brother Alfred at

Maryport in Cumberland shortly afterwards, put it all down to the drink. She wrote, 'you will have seen our defeat in the newspaper. But that will give you no idea of the disgrace of it.' She went on to add that their only comfort now was the hope that bribery might be proved and the town disenfranchised. The letter continued:

> Tom Hounsell said from the *Greyhound* window that it is our friend Legg [the local brewer] here with his taps who has done the job, I do not think you would find a respectable man in the town who could look you in the face and say Warton was in fairly. All Legg's public houses, which is all but three or four in the town, were thrown open free early in the day, the voters fetched hence in Warton's carriages, and when a Liberal went to try and fetch out two of his men the door was shut in face. When the men were sober Rali was far ahead, after that the men became hopelessly drunk and Warton went to the Drill Hall and, as each one came in, he shook hands or patted shoulders and said remember your promise. The state of the streets was something disgraceful, drunken men reeling about in all directions and not only men but [also] little boys and girls. There must have been 150 who promised Rali but [who] voted for Warton, it is a shame that it is possible for a representative of sneaks and drunkards to have a voice in ruling the country.

Warton (or was it the drink?) won by 478 to 469 votes.

Charles Nicholas Warton was Bridport's M.P. for the next five years and he was to earn the sobriquet 'Champion Blocker' for the 'pertinacity with which he objected to bills'. When the House was sitting he kept himself awake in the small hours by taking snuff. On one occasion, however, he dropped off but, old habits dying hard, awoke with a start and a shout of 'I Object!' when the Speaker called out 'The Ayes Have It'. He died in August 1900 aged sixty-eight.

His old stamping ground went reasonably quiet after being absorbed into the new West Dorset constituency. The Unionist (Tory)

LIBERAL CONVERSAZIONE,

Drill Hall, Bridport, Thursday, 2nd Feb., 1905,

[P.T.O.

MR. & MRS. JOHNSTONE HAYE.

26 Mr. Johnstone Haye, the defeated Liberal candidate in 1906, used this card to invite supporters to a 'Liberal Conversazione' at the Bridport Drill Hall on 2 February 1905. Hine Bros., the East Street stationers, booksellers and printers, had a 'Vicar of Bray' outlook on politics: they printed and published cards for both parties.

VOTE   FOR

WILLIAMS,

YOUR OLD AND TRIED MEMBER.

Printed and Published by W. Frost, " News " Office, Bridport.

27 Postcards extolling the virtues of candidates were a 'must' at general elections in the earlier years of the century. Colonel Williams, 'Your Old and Tried Member', played the patriotic part with both the Union Flag and the Royal Standard. It worked. In 1906 he had a majority of 837 over the Liberal's choice, Mr. Johnstone Haye.

28 *Above left.* One of Colonel Williams' supporters at the 1910 general election, according to the card, but it does not say where he is.

29 *Above right.* In the heady aftermath of the 1910 declaration, Colonel Williams is carried shoulder high by his excited supporters and flanked by no fewer than 16 long arms of the local law.

30 *Right.* One of the highlights of the Bridport year was the Allington Fête which always attracted a good crowd including here, on 22 July 1922, the local (West Dorset) M.P., Colonel Williams.

31 General William Booth (1829-1912) speaking from the back of his car near the East Street-Barrack Road junction around 1905. It was his custom on his travels around the countryside to halt outside the town where he was to speak and to be pulled by ropes into the town centre by local members of the Salvation Army. One of the local Bridport officers who helped with the pulling on this occasion was Frederick Cast—and it is a long pull from Stoney Head.

candidate, Colonel Williams, a popular figure in both the constituency and at Westminster, and prominent in the railway and banking worlds, after winning the seat in a bye-election in 1895 with a 1,213 majority, was returned unopposed in the general election later that year and again in 1900, the year Warton died. The Liberals put up Mr. Johnstone Haye in 1906 but the Colonel again won easily with an 837 majority.

Trouble returned with the 1910 election, when mud was thrown at several motor cars and a Liberal supporter pitched a granite boulder through the glasslight and into a crowded Unionist meeting in the Drill Hall. At Whitchurch Canonicorum it was the Liberals' turn to suffer, water being thrown over a speaker through a skylight at the village hall.

But it was not serious all the time. When Mr. W.S. Edwards, the Liberal candidate, employed some of the workhouse 'casuals' to carry sandwich boards around Bridport extolling the Liberal cause, some of the Unionist supporters seized the opportunity and walked in front of them with their own sandwich boards proclaiming, 'This is what happens under Free Trade'. The Colonel won with a record 1,252 majority and the seat has stayed Unionist (Conservative) to this day.

Modern TV election coverage has nothing on *The Bridport News*. With considerable enterprise, its proprietor arranged to have all the 1910 election results sent to his office by telegram and they were first flashed on a screen at the Conservative Central Committee Room in East Street and on the outside of Miss Dare's premises on the other side of the road. The latter proved unsafe in the high winds that were blowing at the time and the screen was moved inside a window. Over 2,000 people gathered to watch the results, considerable cheering greeting each one, especially the 'Gains'. The country results came in later and were shown outside *The Bridport News* office by limelight.

Bribery with drink was not the only questionable method the two parties stooped to during Bridport's last days as a separate seat. As the seat was decided by the votes of local men who paid 'scot and lot', i.e. those who paid local rates or tax, the electoral roll was ruthlessly scrutinised by both parties who wanted to remove as many of their opponents' supporters from it as possible. They were looking for anyone who had not paid Bridport rates for the six months prior to polling day. Dozens of names were removed, often on extremely flimsy grounds such as those of one man who had obtained poor relief to bury one of his children at a time when he did not have sufficient money of his own to pay for the burial. Therefore it was claimed (successfully) that he would have been unable to pay the town rate and his vote was rejected.

THE LICENSED TRADE

Drink *was* plentiful in the town. Like most towns of its size, Bridport had long since had its own brewers, including the Bridport Brewery in Gundry Lane where it had been founded by Samuel Gundry around 1795. There was also Gundry, Down & Co., certainly brewing in East Street between 1817-23, and succeeded by John Legg of West Bay Brewery around 1820, and by Job Legg (Lyme Regis Brewery) ten years later.

Unlike most other towns, however, Bridport still retains its own independent brewery in West Bay Road where Messrs. J.C. & R.H. Palmer's have been in business at the Old Brewery for over a century. This brewery was founded in 1714 when beer was shipped from there via West Bay to London, Southampton and Weymouth. It was then owned by a Mr. Rose who was declared bankrupt in 1812 and the business was acquired by Mr. J. Cole of West Street, who was later joined by Thomas Legg as a partner. They traded as Cole and Legg, but in 1842 Thomas Legg was trading on his own. Job Legg (Bridport Brewery) succeeded him and was most likely the brewer at the heart of the alleged drinking bribery during the 1880 polling day. He moved to West Bay Road where, on his death in 1892, the assets were acquired by Palmer Bros. and the business was renamed the Old Brewery.

It claims to be the only thatched brewery in Europe and its water wheel is the oldest in the four south-west counties. Probably one of the last purpose-built inns in the area is the *Millwey* which was built on the Millwey Rise housing estate in Axminster around 1970. Its licence was eagerly pursued by many bigger brewers but went to Palmer's.

There was a good trade for the brewers in the town, and not just on polling days. It was once said that there were 15 public houses in the half-mile stretch of South Street between the Town Hall and Palmer's brewery. In 1848 *Piggot* listed 31 inns or taverns in Bridport and no fewer than 23 beer retailers, not to mention

32 The *Greyhound Hotel*, East Street, *c*.1904. It was empty for a spell in 1999 but, happily, has been refurbished and is once more a credit to the town.

a wine and spirit merchant and the grocers, most of whom probably stocked drink as well.

The 31 listed inns were the *Cross Keys, Five Bells, Bridport Arms, George, Leopard* and *Ship*, in South Street, the latter said to have had the first skittle alley in the town; the *Pack Horse, King of Prussia, Eagle, Bull, Greyhound, Dolphin* and *Three Mariners* in East Street; the *Plymouth, Lily, Sun, Star* and *Royal* in West Street; the *Golden Lion* in East Road; the *White Lion, Kings Arms,* and *Boot* in Allington; the *Seven Stars* in Barrack Street; the *Crown* in Harbour Road; a second *Bridport Arms* and the *Neptune, Shipwright Arms* and *George* at the Harbour itself; the *Hope & Anchor* in West Street; the *White Lion* and the *Kings Arms* in St Michael's Lane.

There were others, including the *Rook* in West Street and the delightfully named *Hit and Miss Inn* in South Street, both of which are mentioned in auctioneers William Morey & Sons' accounts book, the *Auld Acquaintance* in North Allington and the *White Bull Inn* in East Road, certainly as late as the turn of the century. There had been many others in previous centuries.

The *Greyhound* and the *Bull*, both in East Street, were hotels as well, the rents accruing from the *Bull* being used to maintain a local school. The *Bull* dates from at least 1593, when

there is a reference to the fact that strangers there 'did contribute a shilling to the fund to build a Market House in Bridport'. In 1701 the inn was, surprisingly, bought by a local Quaker, Daniel Taylor. Later he formed a charitable trust which, by means of the rents from the *Bull*, was to maintain a school for 'twelve of such poor children, sons of poor inhabitants of the Borough of Bridport'. For a teacher, Daniels wanted an 'honest and discreet person, skilful and experienced in the art of reading, writing and arithmetic to teach the children'. Such a man would be dismissed if he was guilty of any ill behaviour (such as drinking in the *Bull*?). The *Greyhound* is said to have existed as a tavern on today's site at 2 East Street as early as 1300. It recently closed and its boarded-up windows hardly enhanced the main street. It has now been refurbished.

Daniel Taylor also gave the almshouses opposite the church in South Street in around 1700. Known as the Quakers' (Friends') Alms Houses, there had originally been a house and some tenements there. Taylor, born in a house in West Street that stood on the site of today's Gateway supermarket, also gave the Quaker following a nearby barn which was converted into a meeting hall.

33 & 34 One hundred years after this was taken G.W. Read's shop on the right is Bridget's Market and has grown another storey; apart from a facelift, the *Bull*, seen above around 1900, is basically the same building as when Mr. Knight ran it. He could leave his coach outside without having to worry about double yellow lines or traffic wardens. Below, the popular hotel from a watercolour painted by an unknown artist in the 1970s.

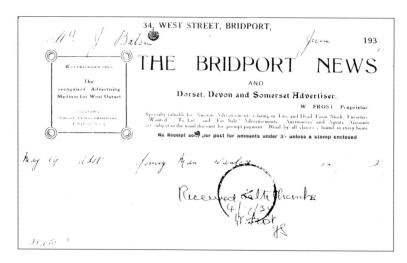

35 *The Bridport News* was a 'must' for local classified ads in 1939 (and still is, of course). For two shillings, J. Balson, a local butcher, has advertised for a 'young man'.

COMMUNICATIONS

Bridport had its own newspaper as early as 1847, when William Charles Frost, the pioneer of the penny newspaper in West Dorset, established a local paper in an office near the Unitarian chapel in East Street. Eight years later in 1855 he launched *The Illustrated Bridport News*. It has changed its name from time to time, becoming, barely six months later, *The Bridport News and General Advertiser*, then, just another six months on, *The Bridport News, Dorchester, Lyme and Beaminster Chronicle and General Advertiser* and, today, *The Bridport and Lyme Regis News*. Whatever its past names, it has almost always been affectionately known as *The Bridport News* and is referred to as such throughout this book. Produced at first in West Street, where the four local pages were printed on a Columbia hand-fed press, the paper remained in the Frost family's hands until 1962, when William Frost's grandson, Wilfred Frost, sold it to the Berrows Group. Then the paper moved to its present offices in East Street although it was actually printed in Salisbury and later Taunton. Today it is owned by News Comm plc and put together on state-of-the-art machinery at Weymouth. It has served its community well.

In April 1883 the Long Distance Telephone Company contacted the Town Council saying that they proposed to place Bridport in direct telephonic communication with London. The Mayor, Arthur Reynolds, wrote to them asking what it would cost and was told, 'Nothing—to Bridport'. By the end of the century the town was, to quote *Mate's Guide*, 'connected by the telephone with all places in the kingdom on the Trunk System, but connections have been established in the town and neighbourhood for subscribers, by the National Telephone Company, whose exchanging office is in South Street'.

FIRES

The decision to ban thatch in Bridport in the late 1700s meant that the town was spared many of the disastrous fires that half-destroyed many others during the 17th and 18th centuries. But there were still fires, notably at Allington in 1796, when a fire that broke out in

> a house used for the reception of strollers, raged with such violence, that the utmost exertions of the inhabitants were insufficient to get it under (control) until twenty-four houses were destroyed, including two public houses, the *Ship* and the *White Lion*.

At least two people, one of them a child, were killed in this fire. Four more perished at Allington in 1840 when part of a burning house fell on them. It was one of 22 destroyed by the second fire.

West Bay was the scene of a fire in the later 1800s, when the post office, several cottages and the local branch of the Somerset Trading Company were all destroyed. The thatched *Bridport Arms* was under threat at one stage and the contents of the upper rooms were removed. Bridport Fire Brigade took 35 minutes to reach the scene, and were followed by two wagon-loads of curious onlookers who help to swell the thousand people said to be there already. Fire struck West Bay again on 19 February 1929 when two houses in Pier Terrace were gutted. The sparks set alight the thatch of two cottages opposite which were also destroyed. Mr. Chorley, the landlord of the *Bridport Arms*, discovered the fire but was unable to contact the police by telephone and was forced to drive to Bridport police station to raise the alarm.

The West of England insurance firm gave the town a gift of a fire engine in 1890. Unlike its predecessor, which had been housed in East Street, the new machine had part of the market

at the Town Hall made available as a fire station. One drawback, however, was that the horses to pull it were still stabled at the *Bull*, thus adding to the call-out time by the requirement to bring them along East Street. Once harnessed, the leading horse, at least, had a rider, the other men sitting behind the driver. One of them was a stoker whose job was to raise steam *en route*, thus ensuring that the pump could be used immediately on arrival at the scene of the fire. He was held in position by a strap to prevent him from being thrown off. All the firemen were elected around the turn of the century.

Bridport bought a Merryweather Steam Pump in commemoration of the Coronation of Edward VII in 1902. Horse-drawn at first, it was later pulled by a Daimler car. In 1926 a modern, six-wheeled, Morris fire engine replaced it. The Merryweather vanished during the Second World War but was later found in a Birmingham scrapyard, brought back to Bridport and renovated. It attended the fire

36 Fire damage at Pier Terrace, West Bay, in February 1929.

that destroyed the West Street Infants School, also known as Mrs. Gundry's School. This attractive, thatched building had once been a malt house, thought to date from the 16th century, but it became a school in 1838. Its first master was a Mr. Bishop, who had formerly run a small school in King of Prussia Lane (now King Street), assisted by Mrs. Hardy. At the time of the fire a Miss Dade was head-mistress. The fire, which took place on 12 November 1906 caused damage estimated at between £300-400 which was paid for by the insurers, Commercial Union. The school's pupils were transferred for a short spell to the Baptist school in Victoria Grove and were later shared among three infants schools in or near

Bridport. The West Street School later became the site of Bridport-Gundry's car park.

The fire brigade became part of the National Fire Service (NFS) during the Second World War and members rendered considerable service during the air raids on Exeter, Plymouth and Southampton. One of its biggest post-war fires was in June 1949, when one and a half acres of the Gundry net works were destroyed and over £250,000 worth of damage was done. This fire was the work of an arsonist who was caught and sent to prison. Costing £700,000 to build and strategically placed at the northern end of the link road in Sea Road South, Bridport's new fire station was opened in September 1996 by the Duke of York.

37 Bridport's Merryweather fire engine at a local fire around 1906. It was replaced in 1926 and, somehow, during the Second World War, it vanished. Discovered in a Birmingham scrapyard some years later, it was brought back to the town and renovated.

38 & 39 Bridport's West Street Infants School was once a malt house. It became a school in 1838. On 12 November 1906 it was destroyed by fire despite the efforts of the fire brigade.

40 & 41 Mopping up in Diment's Court in October 1913 after torrential rain caused 'water and mud to flow like lava off the hills behind it' and bury the court in mud two or three feet deep. Cleaning-up operations went on for days. One of the Borough Council's main priorities was to start a subscription list to help the families with coal to start fires to dry out the houses. But first the insides of the houses had to be cleaned.

FLOODS

Not all Bridport's disasters stemmed from careless sparks. In 1913, after a week of abnormally high winds and rain during which a 'three-mile high' water spout was seen by several people off Eype Mouth, heavy rain throughout the day of 6 October was followed by a deluge in the middle of that night. The lower parts of South, West and East Streets were under deep water as the streams around the edge of the town rose to record levels.

Worst hit was Diment's Court in North Allington, into which 'water and mud flowed like lava off the hills behind', leaving the court under two and a half feet of mud. Other courts in the area were affected but not so badly. Cleaning-up operations took days, several horses and carts being needed to take the mud away. A concerned council deliberated over future means of preventing a repeat; its immediate concern, however, was to start a subscription list to help the stricken occupants, the first priority being coal to get fires going as soon as possible. So severe was the flooding that *The Bridport News*, unusually for the time, carried pictures of the flooded court. Turned into a series of postcards, these pictures were sold at Frost's shop in support of the council's subscription list. The court would be flooded again on more than one occasion, the latest being as recent as the mid-1990s. Hopefully flood prevention work, including the raising of a road, will make that occasion the last.

In stark contrast, it was a shortage of water that upset the even tenor of Bridport's passing days in June 1930, when a water main at Bredy burst leaving the town without water. Some people drew water from a spring in Crock Lane; others, in the Allington area, from another spring at North Mills. Local businesses were able to help, many people in South Street getting their water from Palmer's brewery. Barrack Street residents used a pump at the *Seven Stars*, while in East Street local residents went to a private supply at George's Restaurant, others to a similar source at the *Pack Horse*.

Those people who were unable to get their water from private sources were supplied from the Water Company's premises in South Street by large tanks carried on lorries. Households were rationed to one pail per day.

National as well as local disasters were matters of grave concern to Bridport and, indeed, most small towns in Britain. In April 1912, when the *Titanic* was sunk in the Atlantic, relief funds were collected throughout Dorset for the families of the victims. Naturally the recently formed 1st Bridport Boy Scout Troop was to the forefront with the collecting boxes in the town.

CULTURE

The Literary and Scientific Institute occupied a rather solid-looking building of Portland stone in East Street, where it started out as the Mechanics' Institute in 1830 when its first president was William Forster, a member of the Society of Friends. The leading light behind the Institute was Henry Warburton, Bridport's M.P.,

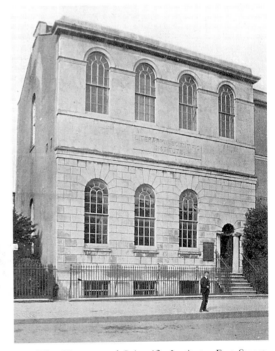

42   The Literary and Scientific Institute, East Street, 1903.

43 Elephants lead an Edwardian circus down West Street.

who laid the foundation stone. After early financial difficulties and closure for some years, it re-opened in 1854 and became for many years an important part of Bridport's recreational scene with a reading room, library, a small local museum and even a billiard table. In later years, and until 1998, it housed Bridport's county library.

There were also more recreational activities for the working class in Bridport, including the formation of the Bridport Horticultural and Cottage Garden Improvement Society, who held their first exhibition in Magdalen Mead in 1854, when 'wagon after wagon came with freight of the family of flowers'. The Melplash Show had already been in existence for eight years at that time, having been formed in 1846. It owes its origins to a challenge that is said to have arisen out of an argument between two local labourers, doubtless already well into their cups in the *Half Moon* at Melplash at the time, as to who was the better ploughman. A ploughing match was the outcome and, although history does not record the result of the challenge, their match became an annual affair and soon developed into the popular, one-day, agricultural show which now takes place on a permanent site near West Bay.

By 1867 there were over thirty classes for horses, sheep, pigs, root crops and corn, though oddly enough, not for cattle. Ploughing was very much to the fore with three classes, and if you used a plough 'of the manufacture of Mr. Brown of Melplaish [sic]' an extra ten shillings was added to the two pound first prize. Such incentives were not confined to the ploughing classes. The winner of the five-pound prize for the best four acres of mangold wurzles was only awarded to a farmer who had bought his manure from a Mr. J.H.Smith.

This increase in recreation for the working class, however, did not extend to the many sporting bodies that sprang up in the town during the second half of the 19th century, most of which were at first the preserve of the middle and upper classes. Association football was the exception. That particular sport, although founded largely in the universities, their old boys' associations and the officers' messes, had been hijacked by the workers long before the turn of the century.

But not golf. That would require two world wars before it was enjoyed as much by the workers as the bosses, a point confirmed by the local club's own admirable history which records that, in 1901, a book about West Bay included a reference to the club and its links being 'resorted to by many of the best families of the town and neighbourhood'. To be fair, few if any of the workers could afford the pound subscription or the time off work to play, let alone the price of a set of clubs. The Bridport and West Bay Golf Club claims to be the oldest club in Dorset, having been founded in 1891 after a meeting held in the Town Hall enthusiastically greeted the proposal. It came to life as the West Dorset Golf Club with a nine-hole green above the cliffs at the western end of West Bay. Problems, not least the threat of coastal erosion, led to a move in 1911 to the present site on the other side of the harbour where, in 1921, the course was extended to 18 holes.

44   Bridport Football Club in 1907/8 at their original ground at Pymore.

45   Tennis at Allington Fête on 20 July 1922 in Downe Hall grounds.

46 Bridport Water Polo Club flourished for many years, the relatively calm water inside the harbour at West Bay providing an ideal venue with plenty of room for spectators. The 1907 team seen here is, back row, left to right: C. Elliott, B.F. Cornick (secretary), A. Gale. Middle: W.J. Guppy, J. Roper (capt.), A.G. Churchill. Front: E.A. Whetham, E.J. Hussey.

47 Bridport Cycling Club was another flourishing sporting institution in the town in the later 19th century and certainly down to the 1930s. It is not known if this is a club meeting or members are competing at a local fête around 1905.

Bridport Cricket Club was formed in 1885, playing at Pymore, and sometimes as Pymore, until 1909 when a move was made to its present Brewery home ground. A handsome pavilion was moved from Pymore with the players. In an age when most teams could boast a priest or two, nearby Uplyme often fielded five. It is not surprising to find that Rev. H.R.W. Farrer was a popular skipper in the cricket club's early days and he was supported on the field by at least two other members of the cloth. When he left for New Zealand in 1910 he was presented with a leather suitcase to mark his captaincy between 1896–1909. Although no longer among the leading clubs in Dorset, Bridport CC has had its moments, particularly in 1898 and 1923 when the MCC sent a team down for two-day games. Unusually, Jack Zealley played in both games. In the 1923 match the MCC were beaten by 23 runs after Colonel A. Douglas steered Bridport to a 231-run total with a fine 78-run knock. At the time the club employed a professional called Warby, whose initials, never mind his Christian name, never appeared in print; but he did take 8 for 59 and then 5 for 68 in the two innings in the MCC game.

48 The pavilion at the West Dorset Golf Club on West Cliff, West Bay, around 1900. The threat of coastal erosion, among other things, led to the club moving to the other side of the harbour in 1911.

49 The fifth green at the West Dorset Golf Club in 1901.

50   Middle-class comfort. Former Bridport Mayor, William Edward Randall, and his wife Mary, relax at their home at Magdala House, West Allington around 1928.

Even older than the cricketers was a croquet club which was formed in 1865 and also played at Pymore. The subscription was five shillings and the club had a black-ball system for vetting newcomers. Obviously they intended to keep out undesirables.

Few undesirables ever saw the inside of the indoor tennis court at The Hyde, a Victorian Gothic country house built by the local architect, F. Cooper, in 1883 for Joseph Gundry on the outskirts of the town near Walditch. Gundry was a good tennis player who had represented Oxford in the University match of 1859. The Prince of Wales, later Edward VII, frequently visited The Hyde and would undoubtedly have had tennis lessons from the resident professional, George Savage. Joseph Gundry was tragically killed in a hunting accident in 1891, and the court declined in use—though it still retained

its pristine appearance. It was later used for roller-skating, flower shows, by the American Army during the Second World War, and seemed set to end its days as a cow shed until it was recently re-opened for real tennis, thanks mainly to the Lottery Sports Foundation and private donations.

Just as were many others, Bridport Football Club was started by the members of the local cricket club as a means of keeping its members together during the winter months. It was formed on 7 October 1885 and played its first match the following February at Dorchester where it lost 5-1. Home matches were played at the cricket field in Pymore where Evershot were the first visitors, losing 3-1. In 1929 the club moved to a ground at the *Crown* in West Bay Road, staying there until 1953 when a second move was made, this time to the St Mary's ground where they still play. As with all football clubs, they have had their ups and downs. Bridport, however, seem to have more ups and, apart from professional outfits such as Bournemouth, Poole, Weymouth and Dorchester, are among the strongest sides in Dorset. They played most of their early football as friendlies, later in the South Dorset and the West Dorset Leagues, with a few seasons in the Perry & District League during the 1920s and again in the 1930s. In 1961 they joined the Western League, dropped down on financial grounds to the Dorset Combination League between 1983-8, and then returned to the Western League where they currently play.

TWENTIETH CENTURY

After celebrating Queen Victoria's Diamond Jubilee in 1897 in style, Bridport entered the 20th century a happy and prosperous town. Apart from the fact that one could buy a crate of a dozen bottles of the local Palmer's BB bitter ale for one and sixpence, full employment in the town meant there was money enough to pay for such pleasures. That full employment was due in no small way to the increase in orders in the hand-made net trade brought about by the Boer War, large orders being placed for forage nets for cavalry horses in South Africa and other military necessities. This prosperity was not matched at West Bay, where the decline in the ship-building industry had seen the population halved to 250 between 1870-1901 and it had become far from uncommon to see 'half dilapidated' buildings.

The 19th century passed away to a muffled peal on the bells of St Mary's Church which began at ten o'clock on a night fine enough to draw out huge crowds to celebrate the arrival of the 20th century. The town band, under band master Harold Shephard, played selections including, at midnight, *Auld Lang Syne,* then *Hail Shining Morn.* There was also the usual night-watch service which began at 11.30 p.m. and was conducted by Rev. H.R.W. Farrer.

There was more jollification in late February when the news reached Bridport that Ladysmith had been relieved. The band was soon out again playing to the excited crowds that thronged the main streets. The celebrations were repeated, even exceeded, in May when the 218-day siege of Mafeking was also ended. Once again the Volunteer Band loyally did its job, the church bells pealed away joyously over the roofs of the town, cannons were let off, and many a happy citizen joined in by 'discharging all sorts of guns all over the town', happily not into the torchlight procession that wended its way around the streets. *The Bridport News* does not tell us so, but it is safe to assume that the pubs did a roaring trade. One Bradpole couple even went as far as having their son

51 First prize for effort. A Carnival 'Best Decorated Bike' class entry from around 1900 prepares to leave home in North Allington.

52 George Elliott's grocery shop in East Street decorated for the Silver Jubilee of King George V in 1935. The building on the right is the *King of the Belgians* inn, formerly the *King of Prussia* but now the *Lord Nelson*. The house on the left was destroyed during a Second World War air raid and the site is now part of the entrance to the East Street car park.

christened Baden after the leader of Mafeking's heroic defenders. Apart from the increase in trade, the town had a special interest in the Boer War in which many of its sons served with the colours. They included John Davis who was injured at Spion Kop, and sailor Joseph Gerrard who went ashore to fire a naval 12-pounder at the enemy.

In 1900 the main streets, South, East and West, were laid with fresh stones which were rolled into the earth by a steam roller. It frightened the horses, who were still competing with the horseless carriages in 1919 when East and West Streets first made the acquaintance of tarmac.

Bridport was *en fête* again in 1911 for the Coronation of King George V. There were bonfires, the biggest on Allington Hill, a special dinner for the over-60s, and the children all received a souvenir mug, a tin of toffee, half a pound of biscuits and ticket for a free ginger beer at the Playing Field, the latter a gift of Palmer's brewery. There was one sour note—two if you count the people living near St Mary's who might be forgiven for being aggrieved when the church bells began ringing at four o'clock that morning. Over one thousand mugs had been ordered, but so many women, and others who were not due them, went up that there were not enough for all the children from the Baptist church who went up last. More were ordered and they got theirs in the end. Twenty-four years later, in 1935, the happiest faces at the King's Silver Jubilee celebrations belonged to the Town Council's workforce— they had all been given the day off with full pay.

53 & 54 Cornick's grocery shop at 10 West Street sold a considerable amount of home-made and famous 'Bridport Jams'. Much of the fruit used was grown in their own local gardens.

55 *Above.* Development at Allington Park began around 1903 when this plan of the sites on offer was produced.

56 *Right.* Bridport from above Allington, *c.*1906.

HOSPITAL

The building of the Bridport General Hospital began in 1912 on land given by Colonel Thomas Colfox, and it was opened in 1915 in place of the much smaller St Thomas's Hospital at North Allington. The new hospital contained 18 beds in two wards as well as two private wards and there was also an operating theatre. In 1931 an extension costing £7,000 was added with a maternity ward with two beds and two children's wards which were able to cope with six patients.

More machine equipment was installed in 1935, including a portable X-ray machine capable of being taken around the wards, and the entire X-ray department was re-equipped in 1948. The hospital was transferred to the site of the old Isolation Hospital in North Allington in 1996. That building, used for housing Vietnamese boat people in the mid-1980s, had catered for tuberculosis patients but was closed and demolished in 1989. The General Hospital's buildings in Park Road are currently unoccupied.

Health reasons were quoted by the council in 1910 when it decided to ban the shaking of mats into the street after eight o'clock in the morning. 'It could lead to illness among the children,' claimed Alderman James, 'and it should be stopped after a certain time in the morning.'

CINEMA

The first moving pictures were seen in Bridport on 26 February 1912, when the Electric Palace was opened in the Liberal Hall, formerly the Old Artillery Hall, in Barrack Street; the first manager was Sidney Sheppard. Its first offerings were six shorts, including *Maiden of the Piebald Indians*, and the children of the town quickly took to the penny matinée on Saturdays. A travelling cinema also visited the town, setting up business in a tent in the Fair Field at the end of South Street where the *Fisherman's Arms* was later built.

The Electric Palace closed in 1926, but reopened eight years later as the Lyric and served the town again until its final closure in

1962 when the last film shown was the Hitchcock thriller *The Secret Partner*. A second cinema opened in South Street in 1926 and was known at first as the New Electric Palace but this was later shortened to the Palace. Unusually it had shop blinds outside.

North Allington resident Mr. Paul brought ice-cream to Bridport when he started selling it from a hand cart outside the Town Hall. Later, in the 1930s, the 'Stop Me and Buy One' Walls ice-cream vendors, on specially constructed three-wheel bicycles selling penny ices, were a familiar sight in the area, especially at West Bay where they competed with the stationary vendors.

PROGRESS

The Bridport Borough Electricity Undertaking's new power station was opened in St Swithin's Road on 30 January 1930. As was usual, a member of the Colfox family, Mrs. Philip Colfox, supported by the Mayor, Alderman Walter Powell, did the honours, using a silver spanner specially made for the occasion. The plant, which had cost £20,000 to build, had already been producing electricity for over a month, but that hardly seemed to matter to the excited gathering that watched Mrs. Colfox 'switch on' the town. The Undertaking served 50 users initially and sent out 185,000 units in its first year of existence. In 1948 it was taken over by the

57 & 58 Mayoral robes arrived in Bridport in the very early years of this century as these two pictures of William Edward Randall indicate. The first picture, taken in his first term as Mayor in 1898, shows him wearing just the chain of office. In 1910 he is seen wearing the robes. William Randall was a local man who was born at Loders in 1847 and attended Bridport Boys General School, where he was taught by John Beard, headmaster from 1854-94. He became a pupil teacher himself but later went into business at the Wine and Spirit Shop in South Street, now the Book Shop.

South West Electricity Board, by which time there were around 6,000 users. A dinner to mark the occasion was graced by the Mayor, Alderman E.J. Rees, and held at the *Greyhound*. Prior to the arrival of mains electricity some buildings in the town—the Palace Cinema was one—had generated their own electricity.

Nearby Seatown did not gets its electricity supply until around May 1939, just in time for the Second World War blackout. Before that it had to make do with candles and paraffin lamps, the oil being delivered to the tiny hamlet and other surrounding villages by Bridport ironmonger Charles Major.

Progress of a different kind was made in 1935 when the first offender for driving over 30 m.p.h. in the town was fined 10 shillings. He was George Lutley Schlater Booth who had been followed from West Bay at speeds of up to 55 m.p.h. and was still doing 45 when he passed the *Fisherman's Arms*. From evidence given in court it seemed that the police sergeant and a constable were patrolling the built-up area looking for such offenders following many complaints. Another 'first' in the Bridport Court that year went to Frederick Curtis, a cook at Marshwood Manor, who was found guilty of not having a white mark on the rear mudguard of his bicycle. Several people had been warned following the introduction of the new law. Fred was the first to be summonsed and it cost him five shillings. History does not record who was the first Bridport man to be summonsed for not having a light on his bicycle.

That same summer saw the installation of lights to control traffic entering and leaving South Street at the Town Hall. They were greeted with less than universal acclaim and people who were ticked off by the police for driving through them when they were on red claimed that there was no warning notice displayed at a distance from the lights. Before the installation of the traffic lights, motorists approaching the junction from the east were

In Memoriam.

THE LATE DR. S. J. ALLDEN,
MAYOR OF BRIDPORT,
At Rest, February 28th, 1904.

(From a Photo by Messrs. ELLIOTT & FRY, of Baker Street, London, and Published by special permission).

59 Dr. S.J. Allden was the first Bridport mayor to die in office when he passed away on 28 February 1904. He moved to the town from Newcastle-on-Tyne in 1894, going into practice with Dr. Hay. A keen sportsman, he was a member of West Bay Swimming Club and Bridport CC. He joined the Borough Council in 1897, becoming Mayor in 1903.

warned by a sign on the first arch of the Town Hall that they were nearing a 'Dangerous Corner On Left'.

Not all the police work at the time was connected with motoring offences. In 1930 Constable Ronald Fudge was awarded the King's Police Medal for arresting a borstal escapee who was firing a revolver at him. Thought to be the first Dorset man to get this medal, he went to Buckingham Palace to receive it from King George V himself.

FAIRS

Another innovation, again not welcomed by all corners of the town, was a four-month, summer extension of opening hours to 10.30 p.m. for local pubs and hotels. Not surprisingly, the churches led the opposition. The pubs did a roaring trade on market days, which were originally Wednesdays and Saturdays. Fairs were held on Old Lady Day, Holy Thursday and Old Michaelmas, and another at West Bay on the Tuesday of Whit week. These were held in the Fair Field in West Bay Road. Until the 1930s the twice-yearly fair was eagerly awaited by a town not yet surfeited by TV and other modern leisure distractions. There were sideshows, stalls, rides and swings, hoop-la and coconut shies and, above all else, the non-stop music and the clatter of the steam engines.

60 Thomas Alfred Colfox, Bridport's great benefactor, seen in a photograph marking his engagement to Miss Constance Nettlefold of Birmingham in 1885.

Until at least the outbreak of the Second World War, Marshall Hill's 'fun city' was the big attraction and there were stalls the length of West Street, as well as a horse fair. For the children the gingerbread stalls were great attractions and also the 'Roll A Penny' stand, somehow more innocent-seeming than its modern equivalent, the one-arm bandit. At one time Allington too had its own annual fair on the first Wednesday in August.

Freddie Sprake's *Cross Keys* inn in South Street was a popular port of call for farmers attending the market but, in an age when the gentle sex was seldom seen in a pub, only men could be found in the public bar. Their wives, however, went down a narrow, flagged passage-way, on the left-hand side of which was Mrs. Sprake's dining room where sherry, the favourite feminine Market Day tipple, was brought through for them. That passage-way also led to the stables where, after being unhitched from their wagons or traps, the horses were kept until it was going-home time.

Another much-awaited annual jollification was, and still is, the town's carnival, which began some time around the turn of the century and has been held, more or less, ever since. Gaily decorated floats wended through the crowded streets and much-needed cash was raised for good causes. The local hospital has been one such cause, especially just before and just after it was built, when the carnival was called the Hospital Carnival. In 1912, for instance, the considerable and then record sum of 70 guineas was raised by the carnival. Eleven years later the carnival raised over £500 for the Alexandra Rose Day funds.

PEOPLE

It was with sadness that Bridport learnt of the death of Colonel Thomas Alfred Colfox on 14 April 1945 at his Coneygar House home at the age of 86. Born in 1859, he was elected to the Town Council in 1887, taking a seat in the North Ward; two year later he became one of the town's youngest mayors and in 1896

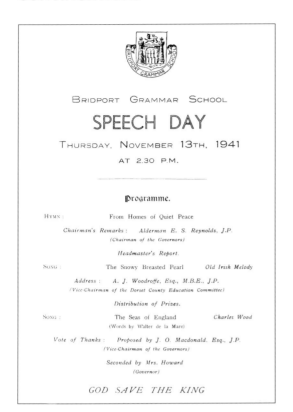

61 & 62 Bridport Grammar School Speech Day, 13 November 1941.

was elevated as an alderman. He served on the council until October 1926. He was a founder member of the Dorset County Council in 1889, became its chairman and served until retiring in 1933. He was also a magistrate, the Deputy Lieutenant of Dorset in 1911, and the county's High Sheriff in 1920 and 1921. But mere titles, dates and length of service cannot indicate the esteem in which he was held by all walks of life throughout the town. His was a remarkable story of service and generosity to Bridport. Almost everybody in the town was in his debt, not least the cricket club with whom he had been a talented player, and the Unitarian chapel at which he worshipped and was a generous benefactor. He gave the land on which the former hospital was built, as well as that for the Bridport (now Colfox) Grammar School, asking that the school be named after his father Alfred, rather than himself. Later he gave the

playing fields in memory of his son David and served as a governor to the school until 1935.

Bridport can claim an interest in the 1870 Education Act, one of the milestones in the march towards a fairer and more just society. Mr. William Edward Forster, Gladstone's man responsible for the Act, had been born at Bradpole, about half a mile across the fields from the Alfred Colfox Comprehensive School. Formerly Bridport Grammar School, this establishment had around 100 pupils in 1918, when the headmaster was Walter Ferris, known as 'Boss', but not to his face. There was no school transport at the time, all the children having to find their own way to the school—many by bicycle, those from Maiden Newton, Toller Porcorum and Powerstock by train, and even one from Chideock on horseback, the horse being stabled in the *Terminus Inn*, just down the road near the railway station. The

63   Allington School seen from the grounds of Laurel House around 1903.

64   Schoolchildren outside Allington School, *c*.1906.

65 & 66   Mrs. Telford's School, Rax Lane, Bothenhampton, 1935.

boy boarders stayed at Victoria Grove, the girls at the headmaster's house in East Street. In 1956 the pupils moved to the Alfred Colfox School and the secondary school became a county primary school.

Walter Trump, one of Bridport's characters, who had been licensee at both the *George* in South Street and the *Greyhound Hotel*, died in 1943. He had learnt the trade as a boy under his parents, who ran the *Cross Keys Hotel*, and served on the Town Council from 1913 to 1929. He was frequently seen outside the *Greyhound* in his shirt sleeves supervising the departure of the hotel's motor bus to the station or of the daily bus that connected with the Waterloo-Exeter line at Crewkerne.

Bridport's Second World War is dealt with in another chapter but, before its real end, which did not happen until the capitulation of Japan, the first general election since

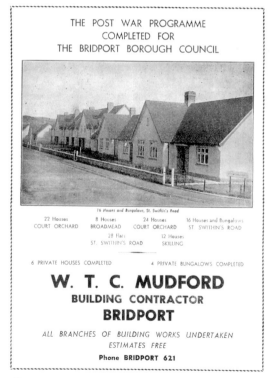

67 W.T.C. Mudford's were responsible for much of the immediate post-war council house-building in Bridport.

November 1935 was held. Voting took place on 5 July. The result was not announced until three weeks later, to enable the overseas Armed Forces' ballot papers to be sent home for the count. The national result changed a Conservative majority of 249 to a Labour one of 146 seats. West Dorset went with the tide in one respect. The Conservative candidate, Major Wingfield Digby, for whom the Duke of Norfolk turned up to speak, was returned with a useful enough majority of 5,184 but, surprisingly, Lieutenant-Colonel Kane, the Labour candidate, picked up 8,215 votes, enough to drive the Liberal, George Newsome, into third place by just over 3,000 votes. That old firebrand Charles Warton would have turned in his grave if he had known that *The Bridport News* quoted all three candidates as thanking their opponents for a clean fight.

The Labour success, locally as well as nationally, encouraged the Bridport branch of the party to contest the first peacetime municipal elections under a red flag, unusually so at a time when almost all rural councillors flew the Independent one. There were two Labour candidates in both the North and South wards: Jack Stone, recently demobbed from the Royal Navy, successful in the North, Arthur Turner, secretary of the local branch of the TGWU, winning a seat in the South Ward. All the other councillors elected continued to stand as Independents.

AFTER THE WAR

Demobilised servicemen did not come home to a town flowing with milk and honey. Austerity ruled the land and although the first peacetime Christmas since 1938 was said to have been a happy one, there was a decided shortage of wine and spirit to bring in the New Year. Once it became known that a local shop had any drink on sale, long queues quickly formed outside and unofficial rationing was introduced.

Also hit was the building trade, where a shortage of bricks slowed down the building of much-needed council houses in Bridport. The first post-war council estate in the town was at Court Orchard, where the first pair of houses was completed in August 1946 two months behind schedule. They were officially opened by the Mayoress, Mrs. Armstrong. By 1953, the Bridport-based builders W.T.C. Mudford had built 46 houses at Court Orchard for the Borough Council, another eight at Broadmead, 16 houses and bungalows and 28 flats at St Swithin's Road, and 12 houses at Skilling.

More housing followed, all allocated on a points basis drawn up with the civil servant's usual love of detail. You got 20 points if you had been displaced by enemy action, 20 if you were living in condemned buildings, 20 if you were an ex-serviceman. Lower down the scale were people already married and still living with parents, or ex-POWs and ex-servicemen and women (15 pts), and overcrowded families (12 pts). Even lower were a man and wife (6), children under 14 (3) and over 14 (6).

In August the first Melplash Show since 1939 was held, and more signs of a return to normality came when *The Bridport News* doubled its four-page wartime format to eight, but at first not for every week. One old friend to go in May of that year had been the Britway British Restaurant which had been opened by Mr. W. McBane, a former Parliamentary Secretary to the Minister of Food, on 24 July 1942. British Restaurants had been opened during the war in towns big enough to ensure a worthwhile trade, to provide the public with meals at reasonable prices outside the restrictions of wartime rationing. It was £376 in debt at the time, the increasing additional restaurant and café facilities on offer in the town and at West Bay finally killing it off. In its four-year life it served Bridport with 172,000 main meals, 229,000 subsidiary meals and teas, and 525,000 hot beverages. The buildings reverted to their W.I. owners.

June 1953 was doubly important in Bridport's history. First there was the Coronation of Queen Elizabeth II to celebrate in the usual Bridport fashion, including more mugs for the children. Three weeks later the new Queen's sister, H.R.H. The Princess Margaret, came to the town as guest of honour at the Royal Charter Pageant to commemorate the 700th anniversary of the granting by Henry III of the first Royal Charter to the Borough. 'Bridport Through the Ages', devised and produced by William Fear, was a witty look at the town's past, and if an occasional deviation from the actual facts was necessary to aid the free flow of the story, so what?

Mary Greenwood, Bridport's first lady mayor and first mayoress, died in November 1967 mourned by all. Born in the town in 1911, she became mayor in 1957, the third successive generation of her family to do so, following her father, Walter Northover, and grandfather, Walter Baker. It was during the latter's mayoralty that the present Mayor's chair was made from Bridport oak. In the very early years of the 20th century Bridport's mayors were provided with robes; prior to that they were only distinguished from their fellow councillors or aldermen by their chain of office.

The steady march of progress brought casualties as well as improvements to the town. The motor car and cheap coach travel finished off the railway, and laundrettes and washing machines killed off many small-town laundries, including, in the 1970s, the Bridport Laundry Company Ltd. in St Andrew's Road. The arrival of a Safeway supermarket on the edge of the town in the 1990s was a shot in the arm for Bridport, but not for those whose living would be affected by the cheap fare on offer. It spelt the end for the very popular town-centre Yorke Food Hall, which closed within a fortnight of Safeway opening its doors.

Perhaps one of the biggest changes of the last three or four decades in Bridport has been the loss of so many old family businesses, some of which had been established in the town for over a century. Some remain, of course. Hussey's bakery in West Street still has the reputation of being a first-class baker's, a reputation that George Hussey enjoyed when he

WILLIAM ELMES, General Draper, & Silk Mercer.

Furrier, ♂ ♂ ♂
Ladies' & Children's Outfitter.

MILLINERY,   GLOVES,
MANTLES, COATS,   LACES,
DRESSES, ETC.   RIBBONS.

CARPET, OILCLOTH, and
LINOLEUM WAREHOUSE.

NOTED HOUSE Blankets, Flannels and
FOR ::: Household Linens.

Gent's Outfitter.

TAILORING in all its Branches.

ALL DEPARTMENTS THOROUGHLY
UP-TO-DATE WITH THE
LATEST NOVELTIES OF THE SEASON

21, East St., BRIDPORT.

68 A 1903 advert in *Mates Illustrated Bridport* for William Elmes' East Street shop.

69 William Elmes opened his general draper's and silk mercer's business at 21 East Street in 1885 and, although he died in February 1909, the business was not closed until 1987.

opened for business at 91 East Street in 1911. The move to West Street was made in 1922. For even longer, much longer in fact, Bridport has bought meat from the Balson family which began butchering in the town in the reign of Henry VIII, when a John Balson had a stall in the South Street shambles. But many other old names that seemed as unchanging as the seasons slipped quietly away from the name boards that line South, East and West Streets. Reynolds' draper's shop in East Street, established as far back as 1787, finally closed in 1995, the site becoming a shopping arcade. Just a few yards away another draper (and haberdasher), William Elmes, opened his doors in 1885, but the business closed in 1987. A great attraction for the children at Elmes was the automatic overhead system which sent the cash to the office and then returned the receipt and change. Also in East Street, Mr. Cox made and sold saddles and harness 'of the best quality' from 1826, possibly in other premises at first, until around the Second World War. On East Street's Barrack Street junction, John Guppy began a grocer's business in 1867 that lasted until the 1960s. There have been many others.

Chapter Three

Bridport's Harbour

Harbours make people think of cranes and chains and they will not want to come because they will fear they will not be able to sleep for the noise.

Bridport Town Councillor Machin, 1935

Throughout this chapter, as indeed throughout this book, I have called West Bay by its modern name except when the reference to Bridport Harbour is a direct quotation. The Great Western Railway coined the name West Bay for the railway station they opened at the harbour in 1884. No doubt they felt it looked better on their timetables than Bridport Harbour and was intended to attract more people to visit and, more to their point, into their trains to get there.

Whatever the reason, the name was soon adopted for the tiny community that made its living from the sea. No one ever suggested adopting Hardy's name for the place—*Deadman's Bay*; perhaps the reasons are obvious. The parishes of Symondsbury and Burton Bradstock could well have objected to the name Bridport Harbour in any case, West Bay actually being shared between that pair until the 1920s, when it officially became part of the larger town.

70 Bridport Harbour in 1835, from an old print.

For the month of September 1935 it became Bridport Harbour again, when the Town Council voted 11-6 in favour of a reversion to the old name. In a surprising about-turn a month later, no doubt a quick reaction to local indignation, the same council voted 14-6 to rescind that decision. 'Harbours' said Councillor Machin, 'make people think of cranes and chains and they will not want to come because they will fear they will not be able to sleep for the noise.' Councillor Clapp disagreed. 'In my time, and I expect boys still do, we said we were going to the Harbour, and then got a good hiding for going.'

We will probably never know if ships ever came as far inland as Bridport, and the tiny river may have struggled since before the narrow confines of recorded history to find a way through the sand to the sea. It is also equally probable that the sand may have blocked a navigable arm of the sea extending almost as far as the church.

The earliest reference to a harbour at Bridport dates from 1280, when a mention is made of tolls 'in the maritime places of Bridport for which the Burgesses paid to the King [Edward I] at the Exchequer twenty shillings at Michaelmas'. The burgesses also claimed possession of the stones and sand there (the land between the high and low tide marks), a right their ancestors had always used.

In 1388 Richard Huderesfield received a grant from Richard II to remake the harbour, which had fallen into a bad state of decay, and he was permitted to make a charge of one half-penny for each horse-load of merchandise either arriving or leaving by ship.

71 The beach at West Bay was a great attraction for all Bridportarians including the ladies of the Hounsell family, seen here around 1906.

72 A water polo match at West Bay around 1910 seems to have attracted more than a few supporters. It is hoped that they did not leap to their feet when their team scored.

Little seems to have been achieved by Huderesfield. In 1392 a second grant was made by Richard, this time to 'the bailiffs of the vill of Bridport' who were told:

know ye that whereas it is your part suppli-cated that since you have begun anew to build a certain port at the aforesaid town, where a port did not formerly exist (?), which would be useful there as well as for the resort of ships as for the advantage of the whole country, but you are not able in any manner to bring to the desired end the work thus at length begun by you, not without great labour and expense, unless you be relieved from elsewhere; we are willing to order to be granted to you some subsidy from the things sold at the port of the said town brought by water and thence carried, to be by you at all times collected, everything sold as portage of one horse at the port, brought by water or carried away from same, one farthing, by you, from the feast of the Purification of the Blessed Mary last past unto the end of three years thence money thence arising be applied towards the building of the aforesaid port and not for any other uses.

At nearby Lyme Regis, men were also fighting a seemingly never-ending battle against the elements to have their own port. In their case they did not have a flat hinterland into which they could dig. They built a port, first of wood, later in stone, in the sea itself. At Bridport the mouth of the tiny river had to be widened and baulked and an inner harbour was dug out. Bridport's would be a battle in which both sides took turns in winning. In 1444 it had been the elements' turn, the Bishop of Salisbury granting an indulgence for building and repairing 'a new port at Bridport Haven for the preservation of merchants and mariners'.

Those same elements held the upper hand nearly two centuries later when the burgesses of Bridport petitioned James I for permission to ask for a collection from the wealthy because they needed as much as £3,000 to remake the decayed harbour. The wealthy were not so kindly disposed to part with their money, however. Only 61 marks (around £40) were forthcoming, and the good people of Bridport petitioned the King for permission to invest

73 *Above.* The need for pilots to steer vessels entering and leaving West Bay is, perhaps, best illustrated by this view of the long and narrow passage that had to be negotiated before reaching the inner harbour.

74 *Left.* Sailing at West Bay in 1903. The Corinthian Sailing Club was formed in 1896 to foster the amateur sport and members had the advantage of a clubroom in the Pavilion. Races were held fortnightly throughout the summer. Thought to be the most suitable type for West Bay, a one-design class with an 18-foot centre keel was started in 1901. Presumably the boats seen here belong to it.

the money instead towards maintenance for a schoolmaster. Permission was granted and the money, along with a few other amounts, was used to purchase some pasture land at Broadoak. Of the interest raised, three-quarters went for the maintenance of a teacher who was to educate four poor boys of the town to be nominated by the bailiffs, the remaining quarter was to be spent in helping the poor.

Men would win the final battle with the sand that regularly choked the harbour. In 1823 sluices were built to hold back the River Brit, the water thus retained being released as and when necessary to scour the harbour free of the sand. It worked, and still does.

Back in 1722, however, an Act was passed for restoring the haven and piers at Bridport in order to 'bring it up to its ancient flourishing state [which] by reason of general sickness which swept away part of its [Bridport's] most wealthy inhabitants, and by other accidents, the haven became neglected and choked with sand'. Nothing much was done until 1740, when Chester-based John Reynolds was hired to build 'two good and substantial piers and two sluices to hold back the waters of the river'. The piers were soon enlarged and the basin made wider. The increased trade brought a useful increase in tolls in its wake. Ships over 10 tons paid a shilling for every ton they carried and the goods could not be discharged (or leave port) until the duties were paid.

But the tolls charged seem still to have been insufficient to maintain the harbour and, on 12 May 1827, another Act received the royal assent. Its aim was the improvement and provision of more security and maintenance of the harbour. It referred to the 1722 Act which had, it claimed, authorised 'the bailiffs and burgesses of Bridport to levy certain tolls on divers merchandise in order to restore said piers and harbour'. It also stated that the

population of the town of Bridport and adjacent neighbourhood whereas of late drew considerable supplies of merchandise, coals and culm, [the] trade greatly increased. If said harbour was [to be] enlarged and improved and additional security afforded to vessels resorting to same, the rates of duties payable by said [1722] Act were not enough to complete the repairs.

The port authorities wanted to be able to charge more. They had their way, and a comprehensive list of the tolls to be charged came at the end of the Act. This list is far too long to repeat here, but virtually every conceivable item needed for everyday 18th-century life can be found there. Among the more interesting are: Ale, sixpence a hogshead against cider's eightpence; Anchors, sixpence per cwt; Apples, one and a penny a bushel; Cheese, two shillings a ton (and there is a lot of cheese in a ton); Cables or cordage (tarred or not), also two shillings a ton; Corn, fourpence a quarter; Livestock was charged at a shilling for a horse, sixpence a cow and threepence for a pig or sheep; Eggs were sixpence a thousand; Feathers, fourpence a cwt (how many feathers did you get in a hundred-weight?). Salted herrings were threepence a barrel, salmon tuppence a kit (a large box or basket). Honey went through at a shilling for a

75 & 76 This 1920s view shows West Bay almost empty of mankind although there are a few vessels around. Below, in 1999, St John's Church looks out over a crowded harbour.

77 The schooner *John Romilly* was launched from the West Bay shipyards of J. Cox on 25 June 1835. Her master was William Swain.

78 Curious onlookers watch a vessel entering West Bay in 1902.

42-gallon barrel, gunpowder at eightpence a cwt, spirits, brandy, gin or rum set you back two shillings a pipe or puncheon (a pipe was two hogshead, a puncheon varied according to the liquor it carried). The dues collected in the first full year (1833) were £5,224.

Many local fishermen avoided the charge, and the duty, on the liquor by having their own private harbours on quieter parts of the coast in which they landed their smuggled goods. In 1832 West Bay was made a bonding port and, with the arrival of bonding and warehousing facilities, it was thought necessary to increase the number of excise men working from the port.

The habit of smuggling was certainly rife on this part of the coast; *The Bridport News* carried reports of court cases against smugglers well into the second half of the 19th century. Earlier that century a 60-year-old blind Bridport widow, Levia Rutledge, had been gaoled at Dorchester for smuggling. Much better treatment was handed out to William Powell, a Bridport stone mason. Gaoled for smuggling, he was released after five months as an act of clemency to mark George IV's coronation. The infamous smuggler Jack Rattenbury, the 'Rob Roy of the West', was caught at West Bay by the Press Gang and taken away to serve, not for the first time, in the Royal Navy. He soon escaped and returned to his native Beer—and smuggling.

There are references to smuggling in the area as far back as the 15th century. Then, however, it was in the opposite direction; cargoes of wool and leather avoided port charges by secretly slipping out from quiet bays for the continent. Not all made it; a reference in 1452 is to one such vessel that was seized carrying goods belonging to merchants from Bridport, Sherborne and Charminster.

It was a busy little port. Towards the end of the 18th century it had 11 ships of its own and took around £400 in harbour dues. Although most commodities entered the town through it, the harbour's main commerce was,

as only to be expected, connected with the rope trade, and vast quantities of hemp and flax from Riga in the Baltic passed through on its way to the mills.

This part of Dorset received through the port the Welsh coal for its winter firing and a significant quantity of Norwegian timber arrived as well. In the opposite direction, as well as the products of the net and rope trade, a considerable amount of butter and cheese, particularly the local Dorset Blue Viney cheese, was sent to London. The Blue Viney produced around Beaminster and Bridport was said to be the best in the county.

By 1797 the harbour had been much improved and was capable of taking vessels of up to 200 tons; it was also a thriving little fishing port. According to the *Universal British Directory* of 1790-8, 'mackrel [*sic*] are here in such prodigious plenty, that there has been set a watch to prevent farmers dunging their land with them which, it is thought, might be apt to infect the air'. There were busy, if small, ship-building yards at the western end of West Bay, turning out many fine vessels including a type known as a Leith smack, so named because they were built for cargo and passenger trade between that Scottish port and London; on at least one occasion a revenue cutter was made at West Bay. The first vessel registered there was the *Adventurer* of 279 tons which was launched in 1779. The largest vessel built was the *Speedy* in 1853. Of 1,002 tons, it was built for the Australian run. During the Napoleonic Wars all but one of 20 naval vessels built in Dorset were launched at West Bay. The *Lilian*, launched in 1879, was, sad to relate, the last ship to be built at the port.

The *Mary Hounsell* was launched in 1833 and plied regularly between West Bay and Newfoundland but was lost by fire in 1844. The second *Mary Hounsell* was then built and also used to carry Hounsell's fishing lines, twine and nets to St Johns where a number of Bridport families had emigrated during the first half of the 19th century. It was the custom of

79 The *Green Fisher* tied up at West Bay around 1908.

the Newfoundland buyers to meet the Bridport manufacturers in the Channel Islands to arrange supplies for the coming season.

We have an accurate but flowery description of what happened at West Bay when a new vessel was launched. A letter written by a J. Friend describes the launching of the *Alfred the Great* at the harbour on 26 June 1852:

> This beautiful ship at Bridport Harbour presented a pleasing and beautiful sight, the vessels in the Harbour displaying their different flags and colours from their masts and rigging; the cheerful faces of the sailors, the men in the shipyard wielding their heavy hammers to remove the bearings of the ship while others were employed in building a cradle for the oak-built monarch for his birth into the waiting elements. Vehicles of every description were to be seen throughout the day conveying elegantly dressed ladies and gentlemen to watch the magnificent scene. Thousands of people were seen wending their way through the fields until the Harbour presented one mass of living beauty. The weather promised fair until half past six when thunder grumbled and at seven rain. The rain increased and lightning flashed but at half past seven the last prop was removed and, as the band played *Britannia*, the *Alfred the Great* glided into the basin amidst the shouts of thousands of dripping spectators.

The ship-building yard closed in 1878 at a time when iron-built vessels were taking over the market and the cost of bringing iron to West Bay was too high. All the slips were walled up and later removed. Three years later West Bay ceased to be a bondport. In the early years of the 19th century the harbour's trade had been at such a high level that the Turnpike Trustees were forced to think about building a completely new road between the harbour and the town, thus saving the long and unnecessary loop to the east as far as Marsh Barn on the Burton Bradstock road. In 1816 the Trustees announced that by so doing they would be 'furnishing employment to the manufacturing and labouring poor of Bridport'. To this end they asked for between £150-200 from the

80   Target practice at West Bay around 1905 with the inevitable curious onlookers.

council towards the purchase of the land over which the road would run. The proposed route would 'leave the Harbour Road at the lake lying south of a field, the property of the late Mr. Symes, from there taking a circular deviation of the back of the hill [Wanderwell]'. The road was cut in 1819. Shortly afterwards, in 1823, Commissioners were appointed to run the harbour, doing so until 1921 when the Town Council took over again.

The railway reached West Bay when the extension of the Bridport branch line as far as the harbour was opened on 31 March 1884. Between 1916 and 1919 the line was closed,

and it was closed again to passenger traffic between 1930-58. The extension was an obvious candidate for Dr. Beeching's hit-list and was closed for ever on 11 April 1964. The following year the rails were removed.

The Esplanade was built in 1887 by Colonel and Mrs. Colfox of the Rax; eight years later the suggestion for a footbridge to be built across the harbour from pier to pier was hooted down. For many years the tiny hamlet was lit by gas but, strangely, there was no lighting on the two piers, and any vessel entering by night was guided by hand lanterns carried in front of them on the quays. They were guided in to West Bay itself by pilots who were rowed out to meet the ships before they reached the harbour.

If, as you must, you discount a small room next to the post office in the Arcade which housed a St Andrew's Mission Church from 1868, West Bay waited until 1939 before it had its own church. It was dedicated to St John and was intended as a chapel-of-ease to the mother church of St Mary's at Bridport. A church at the harbour had first been mooted in 1897, but little was done until a subscription list was started in 1910. The building of the simple, possibly even stark, place of worship began in 1935 on wasteland. It was built by Mr. T. Fowler of Bridport in memory of Canon H.W.R. Fowler, Bridport rector for some twenty years, at a cost of around £4,500. Not unnaturally, there are several maritime features to be found inside, especially in the stained glass, including the miracle of Jesus walking on the water. After the Second World War, a plaque with the names of the six West Bay men who were killed during the conflict

was installed; the clock outside was paid for by local fishermen. At the opening ceremony a lead casket containing that day's *The Times*, an inscribed parchment document, an order of service and a set of the 1935 stamps issued to commemorate the Silver Jubilee of King George V was sealed into the wall.

From fear of invasion in 1940, the beach at West Bay was laid with mines and guarded by anti-tank obstacles and barbed wire; brick pill-boxes were placed at strategic intervals in anticipation of the enemy that never came. Instead it was an invasion in the opposite direction that caused the damage at West Bay, the well-known 'Chapel on the Beach' being damaged during rehearsals for the D-Day landings.

Damage of a different kind was caused in 1943 when the sea wall was breached during a particularly fierce storm and water poured through a 40-foot gap. Among other damage, the Pavilion Restaurant (built in 1901) was destroyed. West Bay has always been vulnerable to winter gales; considerable damage was

81 Rough seas at West Bay in 1905.

82 Damage at West Bay was caused by severe storms two days before Christmas 1927, when a 28-ft. breach was made in the sea wall.

83 Workers struggle to put right the 1927 storm damage.

84 Bridport Swimming Club's changing accommodation escaped the storms. The Club was a prominent and popular feature of the harbour, having been formed before 1900.

85 West Bay was considerably developed around the turn of the century, the Esplanade having been built in 1887 on land given by Lord Ilchester out of funds from the will of Thomas Colfox. The Pavilion, seen here two years after it was built in 1901, contained a 'commodious reading room' which was also used for concerts and other entertainments. There were also refreshment rooms and a covered veranda facing the sea. Unfortunately the building was destroyed by storm damage in 1943 after the sea wall had been breached.

86 West Bay, looking west.

87   Shipping at West Bay, *c.*1912.

caused two days before Christmas 1927, when 28 feet of the sea wall was breached and a considerable length of it had the foundations scoured out, causing it to settle two feet below its normal height. Damage was done to the Pavilion and all the roads at West Bay were covered in shingle and sand, in many places to a depth of two feet. The harbour was in a sorry state in 1945, at the end of the war, and several thousand pounds was needed to put it back in shape.

Moves to have a lifeboat stationed at West Bay were begun as early as the 1890s but nothing ever came of them, although a West Bay Rocket Crew was prominent in the first half of this century. They were supplied with Breeches Buoys which were stored in a boat house at the rear of the Methodist church.

The sea is never far away in Bridport, as those who browse through the town's cemetery are reminded when they spot the grave of Captain Robert Kemball, skipper of the Tea Clipper *Thermopylae*. Known as 'Pile-on-Kemball' due to his desire to sail home as quickly as possible, he married Mary Jane Smith, a Bridport lass, and lived at West Allington. His was a 50-year command, his first received at the unusually young age of thirty-one.

Chapter Four

Churches and Chapels

We hope visitors and local people will come in and look around, and absorb the beauty and tranquillity within ... Above all, it continues to serve its original function, which is the worship of a living God.

John Cann, Rector, 1989, in the Foreword to John Whitehouse's Guide to St Mary's.

There is no reason not to assume that the present St Mary's Church stands on the site of a pre-Conquest building, even if the earliest work found today, mainly in the transepts and the vestry, only dates from the 13th century. After all, if Saxon Bridport was important enough to have a mint, it was certainly important enough to have a church. Cruciform in shape, with an embattled tower, it is mainly in the Perpendicular style, though the chancel and its aisles were rebuilt and the nave and its aisles lengthened in 1860.

88 The two young boys are tucking in at the tea and cake stall at the S.P.G. (Society for the Propagation of the Gospel) Festival at the Rectory around 1910.

89 Rev. A.H. Bowman D.D. giving a talk on 'Missionaries' in the Rectory gardens around 1910.

90 St Mary's Church in 1906. The small shop behind the trap has an advert for Alexandra Oil.

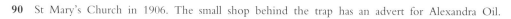

The organ was given as an offering of thanks for the English victory at Waterloo in 1815 and was first placed in a gallery at the west end of the nave. The bells were increased from six to eight in 1887 after having been recast and rehung. One of the more interesting memorials inside is to Edward Coker who was killed at the *Bull* during the Monmouth rebellion.

Much more so than today, a church was historically the centre of its community, in many cases physically so. In St Mary's case, this lends credibility to the belief that the Bridport of the 13th century was centred on the middle of South Street. In those days there would have been very little seating apart from that around the edges where the old and infirm could rest, hence the saying, 'The weakest to the wall(s)'. In all probability the floor was strewn with rushes.

St Andrew's Church, in St Andrew's Road, was built in 1860 in the Early English style. Standing in Bradpole parish at the time, it was at first a chapel-of-ease to Bradpole's Holy Trinity Church. In 1903, however, the land on which it stood was transferred to Bridport parish and it is now a chapel-of-ease to St Mary's.

The foundation stone of St Swithin's Church in Allington was laid in May 1826 by William Elliott. It replaced a smaller building and was in turn thoroughly renovated and given fresh seating in 1901.

The need for a Church House had been long felt in Bridport, but the opportunity to build one did not really arise until 1921 when the property on the north side of the churchyard became available and was bought specifically for that purpose by William Randall, a former mayor. The foundation stone for the Church House was laid by the Earl of Shaftesbury on 29 July 1925 following fundraising which was enthusiastically led by the Rector, Rev. Coulter. Under the stone was placed a bottle containing all the current coins of the realm.

It is likely that the first Nonconformist meetings took place following the ejection of Rev. John Eaton from the Anglican church in 1662. Eaton left Bridport in 1665 and it seems that the Rev. Joseph Hallett continued to preach privately in the area until a house belonging to a Mr. Golding was licensed by Rev. Richard Downe in 1672. In 1742 the Nonconformist minister was said to have Unitarian tendencies and the majority of his flock adopted the Unitarian theology, although some 200 left to form their own Congregational chapter. The Unitarians built their present chapel in East Street on the site of the *Crown Inn*.

The 200-strong rump formed what was first known as the New Meeting, later the Congregational Church, and built a new meeting house in Stake Lane on the site of what later became the Liberal Hall. During the scares and alarms over possible invasion during the Napoleonic Wars a detachment of Hanoverian soldiers was stationed in Stake Lane and their barracks, on the site of the later Public Assistance Institute, caused the change of name from Stake Lane to Barrack Street. In 1860 the Congregationalists moved into a new building in East Street which, with the schoolroom at the rear, cost £3,600 to build. First another schoolroom then a suite of six classrooms were later added and, with the addition of an infant classroom, Bridport was said to have the finest Nonconformist school premises in Dorset.

After the 'split' the portion of the original congregation formed what, not unnaturally, was called the 'Old Meeting'. It moved to East Street in 1794, Sunday Schools being added in 1801. There was a Unitarian Sunday School in existence in 1791 but its records are scanty before the appearance of a minute book dated 1840, which is held in the County Record Office at Dorchester. It was maintained then by Rev. Samuel Wood who was something of an eccentric. He had hoped to build a general school behind the *Seven Stars Inn* which the

91 & 92 *Left and below.* St Swithin's Church in Allington. Built in the Grecian style in 1826, St Swithin's replaced an earlier and small building. Below, the almost stark interior was well lit by gas.

93 Lord Ilchester laying the foundation stone of the Church House on 29 July 1925.

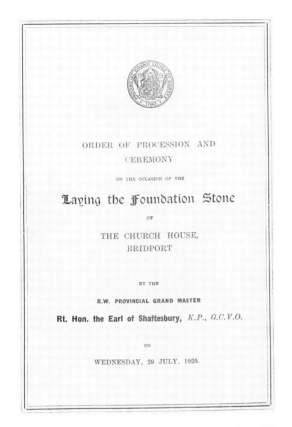

94 *Above left*. The programme for the Order of Procession and Ceremony for the laying of the foundation stone of the Church House on 29 July 1925.

95 *Above right*. Canon H.R.W. Farrer, rector of Bridport 1895–1916, seen here in 1915 at the Rectory.

96 Colonel Williams at Coneygar in 1923 after being presented with a framed portrait of himself by Lady Ilchester on behalf of Bridport Conservatives. The portrait, to mark his retirement as West Dorset member after 28 years (1895–23), was the work of Sir Frank Calderon, a Dorset artist. Colonel Williams also received an album containing the names of the 400 people who subscribed towards the portrait.

97 The Rectory, Bridport, in 1920.

98 The interior of Bridport's Roman Catholic church in Victoria Grove which is dedicated to St Mary and St Catherine. Seen here in 1910, the church was erected in 1846.

Unitarian scholars could use on Sundays, but the extra finance that would be incurred was too high and instead the school was built on the back of the chapel. It cost £360, the money being raised entirely by the congregation, and opened on 16 November 1841. One of its rules forbade the taking of sweetmeats or playthings into the school.

Within a month Robert MacLellan had started a Monday evening class there, with around forty pupils being taught writing, arithmetic and other branches of secular education. The school met for two hours from seven o'clock in the evening, and good progress was reported, especially in writing. The evening school stopped in 1870 when the General School opened in the town.

The chapel, which was closed for three successive Sundays in 1872 when smallpox was prevalent in the town and its neighbourhood, was well known for its treats; the children were taken by wagon, usually to Eype Down, for games from two until four o'clock, then tea and hymns, with everyone going home tired and happy at eight o'clock.

The Catholic church, dedicated to St Mary and St Catherine, was built in Victoria Grove in 1846 with a school. It was demolished

99 Bridport General School, Folly Mill Lane, 1915. Three of the pupils seen here, Thomas William 'Bill' Symes (seventh left, second row), Arthur Abbot and William Gale, went back as octogenarian ex-pupils (and guests) at the school's closing down party in 1990.

100   Girls from the Church of England School in July 1921.

101   The Convent, Pymore Road, *c.*1916.

in 1977 but re-opened around twelve months later. The Convent was built as a preparatory school for boys in 1899. In 1970 it was closed and converted into a retirement home.

Although the Wesleyan movement was to become very strong in the district, Bridport did not have regular Methodist services until 1808 when they were first held in a house at the bottom of South Street. Within 18 months a new site for the chapel had been found in North Street. It was enlarged in 1812 and again

in 1830 before another move in 1838, when the present site of the Methodist chapel in South Street was purchased. A school was added in 1858.

The Baptist chapel on the east side of Victoria Grove was constructed in 1841 to seat almost 300 people; a schoolroom and classrooms were added in 1860. In 1946 the Bridport-born Rev. W.J. Cleal succeeded the Rev. Gilbert Uden as the Baptist minister in the church in which he had been baptised.

Chapter Five

The Staple Trade

To Bert-port which has gained
That praise from every place, and worthilie obtained
Our cordage from her store, and cables should be made
Of any in that kind, most fit for marine trade

Michael Drayton (1563-1631)

It will probably never be known whether flax grew in the fields around Bridport and the rope industry developed in the town because of that, or whether the rope industry was first and the men of the town sowed the plant with its tiny, blue flowers on their doorsteps to save transport costs. Whichever it was, it was the making of the place. And few towns can have remained as devoted to one line of business for as long as Bridport has been to rope and net making. It continues to play a role in the town's economy today, just as it did nearly eight centuries ago when, in 1213, King John issued instructions to the Sheriffs of Dorset and Somerset that:

> We command you that as you love us, your-
> selves and your bodies, you buy for our use
> all the oats you can lay your hands on in the
> Counties of Somerset and Dorset [and] also
> cause to be made at Bridport, night and day,
> as many ropes for ships both large and small
> and as many cables as you can, and twisted
> yarns for cordage.

There have been many subsequent instances when the town's name has cropped

102 A net being made at Edwards Sports Productions Ltd. in 1996.

103 Bridport net workers, 1911.

104 North Mills, Bridport, c.1914.

up in old records. In 1250 it is referred to as a place noted for its cord and hemp manufacturing. In 1352 just over a ton and a half of hempen cord was bought for King Edward III, and conveyed to the Tower of London in five carts. We know from the Exchequer Rolls that it took the carts 12 days to return to London and that the man in charge of the carts was paid sixpence a day. The yarn cost one-and-a-half pence a pound, the trip to London £7 10s. 0d.

Such was the reputation of the town's workforce that, in 1322, six Bridport ropers were sent as far as Newcastle-on-Tyne to instruct the workers there when that newly-founded port started its own rope-making industry and needed someone to teach its own men. Inevitably, Bridport's rope and net-making business attracted rivals, so much so that, during the reign of Henry VII, when foreign imports and even rivals on their own doorstep at Burton Bradstock worried the town, a petition was sent to the King pointing out that the competition could ruin Bridport, especially cheap local competition over which there was no jurisdiction. Some help arrived in 1530 when an Act was passed which prevented the sale of hemp anywhere within a five-mile radius of Bridport except in that town's market.

But the competition remained and increased, rope-making beginning to flourish in the towns and ports with much closer ties to the sea and the Royal Navy than Bridport; towns such as Plymouth, Deptford and Portsmouth, for instance. So it says much for the standard of the local product, if not the local hemp which was now being largely imported, that Bridport's name, fame and share of the trade was by no means diminished. On the contrary, in fact. By the time the 18th century drew to a close the *Universal British Directory* listed among those in Bridport who were engaged in that line of business to varying degrees, staple wool and twine merchants such as Joseph Gundry (established 1665), Sam Gundry junior, Art Gummer, Joseph Golding, J. Coppick junior, Messrs. Gundry and Symes, Seth Seymour, William Hounsell, Joseph Hounsell and John Hounsell.

Kelly's Directory of 1855 lists 27 rope, net and line makers in Dorset. Seventeen of them were based in Bridport, then come Gillingham and Poole with three each. In 1858 *Kelly* gives the figure as 14, but this had increased to 15, despite the almost complete change-over from sail to steam in the Royal Navy, by 1900. Five old firms may have fallen by the wayside, but six new ones had sprung up in their place.

Numbers, if not the trade itself, were soon to decrease. Between 1910 and 1914, William Hounsell & Co., Herbert E. Hounsell & Co., Ewes and Turner, and Richard Tucker & Son all joined forces to become Hounsell (Bridport) Ltd. In the two years immediately following the First World War, Edwards & Sons absorbed Thomas Button & Son and Albert Norman & Son. In 1939 Rendall & Coombes amalgamated with William James and Co., and in 1945 the ensuing firm joined with William Edwards & Son (Bridport) Ltd. In 1947 Bridport Industries was formed from the merging of the Edwards

105   Men at work on jumper looms at Robert Hounsell's Mill at North Allington, *c.*1905.

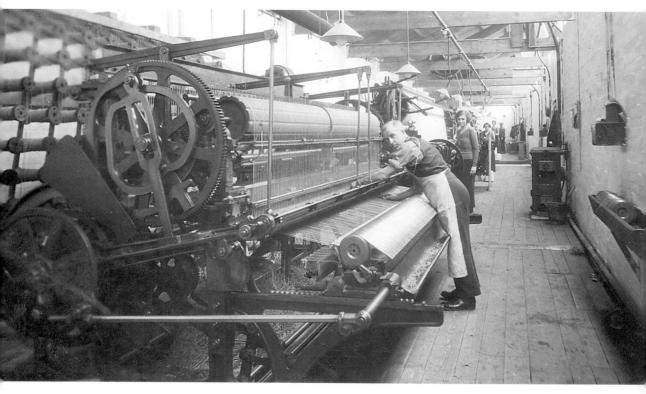

106 Net-making at Robert Hounsell's mill around 1920.

107 Spools of twine in the machine room at Edwards Sports Products Ltd., *c.*1996.

and the Hounsell groups and, in 1963, the remaining independent firms and Joseph Gundry & Co. Ltd. joined with Bridport Industries Ltd. to form Bridport-Gundry Ltd.

Sadly, evidence of Bridport's rope history is no longer physically with us. The old spinning walks and the yarn bartons have gone, victims of the developers' maw which, if it did not actually rip out much of the heart of the old town, certainly ripped out much of its history. Indeed, if it were not for the *Ropemakers Arms* in East Street, the casual passer-by might not even know the town still has a more than slight interest in the trade.

Unlike the rope trade, Bridport sailcloth manufacturers felt the passing of the 'Age of Sail' in the Royal Navy almost immediately. Samuel Cox & Co. employed 2,000 people in their sailcloth factory at Bridport at the time of the French Revolution. Even as late as 1835 there were still four firms engaged in that line of business in the town; ten years later there were only two.

It was, perhaps, unkind that a town which did much for Britain's naval war efforts should suffer from a war. But, in June 1855, during the Crimean War, the eventual arrival of the *Die Partzen* from Memel with a load of hemp was the first such cargo for over a year. Hardship had been felt in the town, especially among those in the trade's labour force who worked from home. The numbers of such 'outworkers', as they were known, have dwindled considerably, although there are still a few of them around.

Today ropes arrive ready made in Bridport, mainly from Asian countries, but nets are still made locally, Edwards Sports Products buying bales of local-made netting and cutting it to size. They can offer Bridport cricket nets, Bridport tennis nets and Bridport indoor sports

nets of all kinds and they supply all the netting and the canvas screens for Wimbledon and football nets for the top end of the market. Sadly for a town which can boast of William Brodie, the inventor of the football goal net, as one of its sons, the bottom end of that market now comes from Korea on grounds of price. Not everyone, however, wants to go to the bottom end of the market. So high is the reputation of tennis netting from the Edwards factory in Bridport that the name is still regarded as the trade brand leader in the USA, probably the biggest tennis market in the world.

And the world was watching on TV when Bridport netting played its part in England's finest sporting hour, in 1966, when Germany were defeated 4-2 after extra-time at Wembley

108 Outworkers net braiding in the 19th century, as seen by the artist on the panels above the Mayor's chair at the Town Hall.

109 James Cornish, the manager, and his family stand in the doorway of the Bridport Gas Company's showroom; the works are seen to the left behind the assembled staff. The building is still there even though gas production in the town ceased as long ago as 1958.

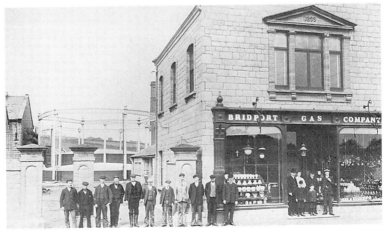

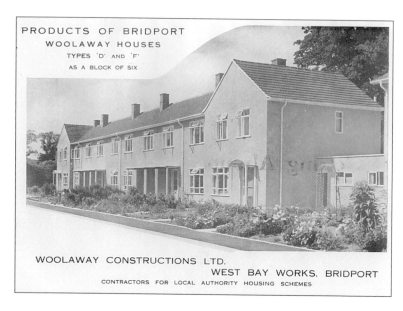

PRODUCTS OF BRIDPORT
WOOLAWAY HOUSES
TYPES 'D' AND 'F'
AS A BLOCK OF SIX

WOOLAWAY CONSTRUCTIONS LTD.
WEST BAY WORKS, BRIDPORT
CONTRACTORS FOR LOCAL AUTHORITY HOUSING SCHEMES

110 Woolaway housing as seen in a 1953 advertisement.

in the football World Cup final. Special goal nets had been made for all the grounds on which the tournament's games were played. All were manufactured from special polythene and, apart from those at the actual joints, no knots were allowed in them. They were erected on site at the various grounds by Bridport-born Ron Croad.

It is no longer just the Royal Navy that still uses Bridport ropes and nets. Today the Royal Air Force is a big customer for camouflage nets, underslung netting used by helicopters, and other kinds of rope and netting. All three branches of the Armed Forces took Bridport's famous products with them to the Falkland and Gulf wars, and they have also been used in space shuttles.

There have been other industries in the town, most notably at West Bay, to where Woolaway Constructions Ltd. moved in 1946 on a five-and-a-quarter-acre site bought by the Town Council for £1,250 and leased to the firm for £70 per annum. They produced pre-stressed and reinforced concrete building units for many years, flourishing in the 1940s

and 1950s when post-war demand for such buildings was at its height. They also made garages and industrial buildings. Some housing in Bridport itself, on the Court Orchard estate, was manufactured in sections at the West Bay factory and erected on site in the early 1950s. These houses fell foul of 'concrete cancer' and were replaced in 1992. Through Woolaway's, Bridport has links with Coventry Cathedral, the firm supplying the nave columns when the bomb-damaged building was rebuilt after the Second World War. Building inevitably went up-market, and the business closed in 1972.

Another West Bay connection with the building trade was the collection of small gravel from the beach. This was carried by coasting vessels to ports around the British coast and abroad for use in pebble-dashing. Fears of erosion finally put an end to what had been a flourishing industry. An earlier use made of the shingle at West Bay had been as ballast, *Mate's Illustrated Guide* claiming in 1902 that thousands of tons were being constantly removed for this and other purposes.

Chapter Six

Getting About

The new bypass will mean many less [sic] accidents, many less [sic] injuries and much less misery.

Roads Minister Peter Bottomley, 1988

G.K. Chesterton's rolling English drunkard may have made the rolling English road, but he did not make them very well. Travel from the Middle Ages, at least until the 18th century, was a pretty frightful experience, and not just because of highwaymen. By the 18th century the once-excellent Roman roads had enjoyed a 1,300-year slumber. They were rough and rutted, dust bowls in summer, seas of mud in winter, and it took ages to get from one place to another. The Turnpike Trusts Acts and a man called Macadam gradually changed all that. Formed to improve the roads in their own respective areas, the Turnpike Trusts did so with monies raised from letting out the rights to make a charge at the toll-gates. These were placed at strategic positions around the towns in the areas for which the Trusts were responsible.

Bridport Turnpike Trust's authority extended as far as Penn beyond Charmouth in the west; beyond that the roads came under Axminster Trust. To the east the area was bounded by the Dorchester Trust. Formed in 1797, the Bridport Trust usually met in 'the new Guildhall' in the early years of the 19th century, but sometimes it gathered at local inns including, on one occasion in 1813, the *Blue Ball* at Loders. But it was not the excellence of the fare on offer there that attracted them. Improvements to the road at Stoney Head Hill were on the agenda and the Trustees obviously wanted to hold a site meeting. They agreed to take up £200 for the work—later this was increased to £250—and Richard Sprackling, their foreman, was instructed to 'begin and complete the improvements with all possible dispatch'. The work included the removal of Henry Saunders' house at the foot of the hill four feet to one side to allow for the road to be widened at that spot. Sprackling was obviously highly regarded by his employers; on more than one occasion they gave him a bonus including, in 1812, £5 as 'a reward for his services and in consideration of the dearness of the times'.

There were toll-gates at the east and west ends of the town, another in South Street, one at Bradpole, where a cottage was built for the gate man in 1814, and a fifth on the Salway Ash Road, which was improved in 1828 when, on 5 April, an Act of Parliament for 'Making and maintaining the Turnpike Trust road at Allington through Broadwindsor and Drimpton to the Crewkerne Turnpike' received the royal assent. The Act continued

111 East Street, looking west, *c.*1901. Of great interest here is the paved crossing place, necessary in wet weather when the street would have been a sea of mud. Look at the man casually leading his horse towards the Town Hall without a care in the world.

112 East Street, looking east and taken at the same time as the previous picture. E.H. Gilbert, second left at no. 15, was a leading furnishing establishment in the town which did all its own cabinet and upholstery on the premises under 'most careful supervision'. They told the world at large that 'All kinds of bedding [was] purified and re-made by the most up-to-date and hygienic methods'.

that 'said road was to be amended, widened, improved, repaired and made Turnpike [standard] between the town and harbour of Bridport in the county of Dorset and the towns of Chard, Crewkerne and Taunton'. The Trust was empowered to put up toll-gates, toll-bars, turnpikes or sidegates and, where necessary, take in garden spots of up to an eighth of an acre.

The tolls to be charged for this new road were also laid down in the Act and it is safe to assume that they were the same for all the Bridport gates. A horse or beast drawing a coach, stagecoach, chariot, landau, chaise, carriage, calash, hearse, phaeton, chair, caravan, van or taxed cart paid a shilling. A horse, mule or ass, whether laden or unladen, just two pence. A horse or beast drawing a wagon with wheels of up to four-and-a-half inches would cost you one shilling and sixpence, with wheels between that and six inches it was one and three, over six inches and it was a shilling

(which seems the wrong way around to me). For a drove of oxen or neat cattle you paid tenpence per score, for calves, swine or sheep only sixpence. Pay once and you had paid for the rest of the day and at all of the Bridport gates, unless you were driving a horse-drawn chaise when a separate toll had to be paid for each new hiring. Really important people— the King and his family, M.P.s (of course), the mail coach, the military and ministers of acceptable religions going to funerals or visiting the sick—were allowed free passage.

The toll-houses were substantial buildings, the Trustees' minute books referring to the use of Purbeck stone floors and deal boards when Bradpole builder William Hide was employed to carry out repairs to the house at the West Gate. The Trust were also responsible for the cleanness and general welfare of the main roads that passed through Bridport, scraping them between the east and west bridges. In the town they owned the public weighbridge at the

113 Stranded motorists are trying to dig their cars out of the snow in this January 1937 *Daily Telegraph* picture. The narrow road that twists away to the left in the background is today's A35, heading for Dorchester beyond Askers.

114   An Edwardian wedding for the Hounsell family.

Town Hall and raised more cash by offering at an annual auction the right to make a charge for its use. Eventually the Trustees approached the council for help in scraping the roads, suggesting, with some justice, to a Vestry meeting that an appropriate number of labourers should be supplied from the workhouse when required. If they were not forthcoming the Trustees told the council they would charge them £40 a year for having to arrange to get the work done themselves. The workhouse had been built in St Andrew's Road in 1836, for 250 inmates, so there was plenty of labour available.

Edwardian pictures of Bridport show a stone crossing place just below the junction of South and West Streets where, by coincidence, there is a light-controlled crossing today. There may have been others or, more likely, simple crossing places through the mud kept clean by sweepers.

The Bridport Trust was unusual in that Stephen Graves (sometimes written in the Trustees' minute book as Grave) was almost always the highest, and therefore successful, bidder for the East, West and South Street gates. Elsewhere (Axminster is a particularly good example), the right to collect the tolls was held by several different people in just one or two decades. The Axminster Trustees often had problems getting their money, which could be the reason why Graves was the regular holder of the toll rights at Bridport. He was reliable. And he was crafty. Few of his bids were rounded off to the nearest fifty or hundred pounds. Instead, with bids such as £402 and £501, he was often one pound higher than the next best bid and thus got the contract. The bids reflected the volume of traffic using the gates, which would, of course, determine the amount of income the successful bidder could expect. At a time when the gates at each end of the town on the main coaching road were going for around £500 per annum each, Graves was successful in winning the South (Street) gate contract for £120; it only took harbour traffic and a small amount bound for Burton Bradstock. It was probably because he was trustworthy that the Trustees allowed him a £20 refund on each gate in 1813 to make up for the loss of trade and traffic when the town was virtually cut off by 'a long snow'.

Sometimes the bidding failed to reach the reserve, such as in 1816, when the Trustees were forced to ask Stephen Graves to collect tolls on their behalf until an acceptable bid was received. He was paid seven shillings a week during that period.

All the Trustees had to take the oath regulated by an Act of Parliament. In the first quarter of the 19th century at least 25 are named in the minute book: Nathan Bourne, Gregory Browne, William Colfox, Rev. John Colmer, Daniel Down, Joseph Down, Elias Dunfield, William Fowler, William Fowler (junior), William Goad, John Golding, John Golding (junior), Bouden Gundry, Joseph Gundry, Thomas Hounsell, Peter Kenway, John Pitfield, Simon Pitfield, Rev. Gregory Raymond, Charles Read, John Salter, William Stevens, Joseph Stone and Robert Strong. But even with so many members, there were often none present at the monthly Trustee meetings and the secretary, after laconically recording the fact, went home. This failing was no by means peculiar to the Bridport Trust. Their western neighbours at Axminster once went seven months without anyone turning up to a meeting and the problem no doubt existed throughout the country.

Exempt from the toll charges, the passenger-carrying Royal Mail coach from Exeter and Falmouth, bound for London via Dorchester, Blandford and Salisbury, left the *Bull* at 2.20 p.m. every afternoon in 1800. It was followed by *Celerity*, a privately-owned coach, at 8.30 p.m. in the evening, except on Sundays. In the other direction, both coaches

left in the mornings, the *Celerity* at 9.15 a.m., the Royal Mail two hours later. The coach from Southampton via Axminster and Honiton left at 3.15 p.m. on Tuesdays, Thursdays and Saturdays; in the other direction, it left the *Bull* on Mondays, Wednesdays and Fridays at 11.15 a.m. in the mornings. Bridport was also at the end of a Royal Mail route which journeyed daily in both directions, via Crewkerne, to Taunton.

Just north of Beaminster, on the A3066 Crewkerne road, the coach faced what the *Dorset Chronicle*, reporting on the opening of Horn Hill Tunnel at Beaminster, called 'that tremendous declivity' (Horn Hill), and added that it had 'hitherto been an effectual barrier to all facility of communication between the lower portion of Dorset and a considerable district of Somerset, especially Bridport Harbour, a difficulty that long seemed insurmountable'.

Originally the road climbed out of Beaminster to the east of the present road. A new road through the tunnel would cut out the tremendous haul over Horn Hill and shorten the route by about a mile. The tunnel's first sod was cut on 12 April 1830 and officially opened just over two years later, on 29 June 1832, amidst scenes of some conviviality after a procession of people from all walks of life, half a mile long and 9,000 strong, walked or rode through it in both directions. The gentry went first, the workmen, one of whose number had been killed during the work, last. Bridport sent its band—and quite a few ordinary people had a day out.

Ten years later, in 1840, the road to the west was also much improved between Charmouth and Penn when the Charmouth tunnel was built. Today, of course, the modern A35 bypasses both Charmouth and its tunnel. Back in 1812, a completely new road between Bridport and Axminster had been proposed by the Turnpike Trusts of the two towns. It never came about, which is a pity because it would have obviated the need for the Charmouth bypass and the proposed controversial bypasses

115 A 1921 sale notice for land at Bottom Farm, Powerstock. Like almost every such sale of the time, it was held at the *Bull*.

116 This postcard bears the inscription 'The Bessco OHT Barn Band'. They are in front of Downe Hall around 1922.

WEST DORSET

Valuable Freehold Sheep and Dairy Lands with Possession on Completion of Purchase,

Situate in the Parish of Powerstock, 4 miles from Bridport, 6 miles from Beaminster and 10 miles from the County Town of Dorchester.

MESSRS.

R. & C. SNELL

Will offer for SALE BY AUCTION, at the

BULL HOTEL, BRIDPORT,

On WEDNESDAY, DECEMBER 14th, 1921

At 3 p.m. precisely, all those EXCELLENT

DAIRY & SHEEP LANDS

BEING PART OF

BOTTOM FARM WITH TWO COTTAGES & GARDENS

IN THE FOLLOWING LOTS:

LOT 1. Part of BOTTOM FARM, comprising Rich Pasture and Fertile Arable Lands, extending to **48**a. **3**r. **30**p.

LOT 2. A similar BLOCK OF LAND, comprising **30**a. **2**r. **19**p.

LOT 3. TWO STONE-BUILT COTTAGES with GARDENS.

POSSESSION OF THE PROPERTY WILL BE GIVEN ON COMPLETION OF THE PURCHASE.

Further particulars may be obtained of the AUCTIONEERS, Axminster; Messrs. TUCKER, LAKE & LYON, Solicitors, 74, Great Russell Street, Bloomsbury Square, London, W.C.1; Messrs. MAPLES, TEESDALE & Co., Solicitors, 6, Frederick's Place, Old Jewry, London, E.C.2; Messrs. TROWER, STILL, PARKIN & KEELING, Solicitors, 5, New Square, London, W.C.2; or of

MESSRS. ELLIS, SON & BOWDEN,

Land Agents, BEDFORD CHAMBERS, EXETER.

JAMES TOWNSEND & SONS, PRINTERS, LITTLE QUEEN STREET, EXETER.

117 This is an interesting picture. Taken by the well-known Bridport photographer Hare on 1 April 1914, it shows a sign indicating that there is a 'New Road to Exeter' over the Brewery Bridge. But surely Bridport's mid-town traffic problems were not sufficient to warrant sending traffic leaving West Bay around the town through narrow and almost certainly unpaved lanes in the direction of Eype?

118 The King Charles Stone in Lea Lane which marks the spot where the fugitive king turned and avoided his Roundhead pursuers. Post-war development led to the stone being moved a short distance.

for Chideock and Morecombelake. This new road was intended to leave the main road out of Bridport just to the west of West Mead, turning sharply north-west and, passing well to the east of Symondsbury, running through the Marshwood Vale as far as Denhay. There it would loop back south to skirt Wootton Fitzpaine and, passing Meerhay and Bowshot, cross the Crewkerne Road above Axminster and run down to that town. It would not save any mileage—from Bridport to Axminster was 12 miles by both routes—but, until the climb up to Monkton Wyld, the new road followed flat, stagecoach-friendly terrain. If such a road were proposed today, of course, every environ-

mentalist in the country would be setting up home in protest camps along its entire length.

Other coaches used the roads, but the most popular image of the time is of the mail coach dashing along with its horn blaring to warn the toll man to open his gates and let it charge through unhindered. Mail coaches never paid the toll, an advantage that other commercial road users often complained about. Bridport's mail came and left under four different headings—London letters, country letters, cross-post letters and bye-letters. The first group is self-explanatory: such mail went direct to, or came direct from, the capital. Country letters passed through London on their

119 & 120 This view looking along West Street is dated 1906 in pencil on the back. But a date *c*.1912 is more likely to be correct. In the other view (below), which looks in the opposite direction, the trees are much younger, and that picture cannot be much earlier than 1906.

way to their final destination, say Bridport to Norfolk. A cross-post, as the name suggests, was for mail that went direct across country from one provincial town to another without touching London: Birmingham-Bristol, Hull-Liverpool, Bristol-Exeter and many others. Bye-letters travelled along the main coach runs between towns without getting as far as London, from Bridport to, say, Blandford.

Being on the main Bridport-Taunton cross-post, Beaminster received most of its mail from Bridport by the mail coach. The other outlying villages under the control of the Bridport office were served by foot-posts who, in all winds and weathers, walked out of the town daily with the mail. The postal traffic in those villages was not usually enough to warrant their having a post office, so instead they had a receiving house. This was either a private house or shop, often an inn, at which letters could be left (received) for collection by the foot-post. The service was known as the Bridport Penny Post. It had nothing to do with the universal charge of one penny for a letter delivered to any address in Britain that was introduced by Sir Rowland Hill. That came later in 1840. Before the Penny Black stamp arrived the cost of sending a letter was based on the number of miles it had to travel, with the charge decreasing pro rata as the distance the letter was carried increased. In other words it cost around 5d. to send a letter from Bridport to Dorchester, but only 10d. to send one to London.

The Bridport Penny Post (the whole country was covered by penny posts and not just Bridport) took its name from the penny charged to carry a letter to the Bridport office where it could enter the mainstream mail service. The penny was collected at source and the envelope was usually, but not necessarily, handstamped to indicate that a charge had been made.

Bridport's first known post office was at 17 East Street in premises now occupied by the Midland Bank. It was conveniently close to and opposite the *Bull*, Bridport's staging post. On 23 July 1890 it moved to No. 12 on the other side of the road, later John Menzies but recently taken over by W.H. Smith. Postal traffic in the town was to increase by some 70 per cent in the 20 years following the move and this, along with the added work for counter staff brought about by the introduction of the Old Age Pension Act, saw a second move to larger premises, this time to West Street. The post office on the site of William Morey's cattle sale yard, at the junction with Victoria Grove, first opened its doors on 3 September 1913. In July 1971 a fourth move was made to premises at Granville House, a stone's throw away in West Street.

The foot-posts, after their deliveries, collected the mail from the receiving houses in the villages in the afternoon in time to take it to Bridport to meet the mail coaches. Some of the foot-posts did not have enough time to return to Bridport and walk back again for the afternoon mail and they stayed in their particular village until collection time. Shelter was not hard to find: a friendly farmer's barn, the receiving house itself, some even had small huts built for them, although there is no record of any of the Bridport foot-posts being treated so kindly. In later years the mail cart, often pulled by a donkey, became the forerunner of today's motorised postman.

The horse-drawn mail cart from Bridport to Lyme Regis was replaced by a motorised service in 1910, at around which time the Dorchester mail was switched from the railway to the roads. Bridport man George Bonfield had both contracts. His man had to leave Dorchester at three in the morning, reaching Bridport an hour later; the return journey was made at seven in the evening. In time, although not immediately, the faster service meant that Bridport's public had an extra half-hour in the evenings for its last posting. The mails still go to Dorchester by road even if, in 1946, severe frost and snow in February forced it back on to the train for a short spell.

TELEPHONE No 25.   CUSTOMERS' CARS GARAGED AND DRIVEN BY OUR STAFF AT OWNERS' RISK.

BRIDPORT ENGINEERING & MOTOR WORKS, 66 WEST STREET,

BRIDPORT, *May 31*   193 **3**

Mr R J Balson.

Dr. to

GEORGE BONFIELD & SON

MOTOR ENGINEERS & HAULAGE CONTRACTORS.

May 2 .	1 Gall Petrol	1	5
4	1 -	1	5

121 Happy days! George Bonfield sold petrol at 1s. 5d. a gallon from his works at 66 West Street in May 1933; later in the month it went down in price. Local butcher Mr. R.J. Balson was able to hire a van for meat deliveries to Symondsbury, Higher Eype, Down Hill and Eype for just five shillings.

122 Gough's Cave at Cheddar was a popular destination for George Bonfield's 1920s charabanc outings. Photographs of the party were almost obligatory and, as with this group of Bridportarians around 1928, a sign was always put on the running board and the charabanc always faced the right.

The receiving houses served from Bridport included West Bay, although, as befitted a port however small, this later became a sub-post office in its own right; Askerswell and Loders (the same man probably covered both); Whitchurch Canonicorum, which was later served from Charmouth; Bradpole, Symondsbury, Burton Bradstock, Chideock, Shipton Gorge and Puncknowle. Long Bredy and Litton Cheney had their mail brought from Dorchester.

In 1797 letters for the London mail coach had to be at the post office by 10 a.m., and for the West (Exeter, Plymouth and Falmouth) by two o'clock in the afternoon. Bridport, being on the main mail coach run, had its mail collected every day. By 1830 the London mail arrived daily at 11.30 a.m. and left at 2.30 p.m. The mail from the West reached Bridport at 2.30 p.m. and left at 11.30 a.m. For Taunton, the departure time was 8.15 a.m. in the morning; it came in at 5.30 p.m. in the evening. The London-Exeter-Falmouth mail coach was usually timed to arrive at Bridport before the departure of the Taunton coach.

The town was well served by passenger coaches, two for London and two for Exeter passing through Bridport in addition to the mail coach. The London to Exeter wagon passed through the town on Mondays, Wednesdays and Thursdays and, on the same days, the return coach was also in Bridport where the coach company's local agent was the aptly-named Joshua Carter. The principal posting inns were the *Bull* and the *Golden Lion*; all coaches stopped at the former.

The modern Christmas-card image glamorises the mail coach, which was seldom glamorous at the time: uncomfortable, bumpy, dusty, little leg room and what sleep could be had all too often interrupted by middle-of-the-night stops to change the horses. Not even the prospect of being shaved on arrival at Axminster by a lady barber could make up for the discomfort. Even less glamorous, but more enduring as it turned out, were the carriers and their horse-drawn carts which, once you

left the main coaching runs, were the life blood of rural England's commerce. They plodded out into the countryside around towns such as Bridport until after the First World War, when motorised transport finally killed them off. A criss-cross of carrying routes had evolved down the centuries; most towns were connected with their immediate neighbours and enjoyed being on at least one long-distance route.

London-bound goods left Bridport's East Street every evening at nine o'clock on vehicles belonging to Russell & Co. Russell also operated from the *Bull* to Exeter, Plymouth and Falmouth, leaving at two o'clock every morning. It is not clear whether or not this was a separate run or a London-Falmouth long-distance run that changed coaches and horses at Bridport, though probably the latter. Other carriers operating from the town included Robert Geng, to East Coker and Bristol from the *Bridport Arms* on Saturday; John Purrt, who went to Chard leaving from the *Pack Horse* twice weekly; John Willmott, to Crewkerne from the *Greyhound* on Saturday; William Coombes, to Dorchester from the *Pack Horse* on Mondays and Saturdays, and Poole, also from the *Pack Horse*, on Mondays; John Dillen, from the *Pack Horse* for Lyme Regis on Saturdays; Robert Tapscott for Weymouth, again from the *Pack Horse*, on Mondays and Thursdays; and a Mr. Hawker who went to Yeovil from the *Pack Horse* on Wednesdays and Thursdays. There were also more local services to such places as Abbotsbury, Puncknowle, Whitchurch Canonicorum and Fishponds Bottom.

Bulkier loads travelled by the vessels which plied along the coast as far as London, with several coasters making the trip from West Bay to Carron Wharf in the Isle of Dogs. Leaving at roughly 10-day intervals, the following vessels made the London trip: the *Prompt* (Richard Freyter, master), *London* (John Foss), *Liberty* (James Gregory), *Alice* (Thomas Fudge), *Bridport* (Joseph Follett) and the *Ellen* (Henry Foss).

123 Downe Hall takes its name from its builder, a Mr. Downe, a London shipping magnate with connections with the shipbuilding yard at West Bay. It is said that the house was built so he that he could see West Bay from it.

124 This postcard view of East Street station has to date from before 1904, as the attractive thatched building was demolished in that year when the station was rebuilt. The danger to the thatch from sparks from passing trains must have been uppermost in the minds of the authorities at the time. The new station has long since been removed.

There was also a weekly service to the Channel Islands by the *William IV* (William Gibbs), to Plymouth weekly by both the *Lively* (William Daniels) and the *Georgiana* (John Manwell), and to Portsmouth twice weekly by the *Liberty* (John Gregory).

Towards the end of the 19th century horse-drawn omnibuses made their appearance, most of those plying out of Bridport doing so from the *Bull*. There was a Monday-Saturday service to Lyme Regis at 3.30 p.m. which returned the following morning at 11.00 a.m. from the *Royal Hotel* in Lyme. Another service to Beaminster and Crewkerne left Bridport at 9.30 a.m. from Monday to Saturday and arrived back around 2.30 p.m.

Railway mania swept the country between 1840-80; if a town had a railway line its neighbour wanted one too. The result was often that a line which never paid was taken over eventually by a bigger rail company and, in the fullness of time and by courtesy of the common sense of the much (and usually wrongly) maligned Dr. Beeching, was belatedly swept into the dustpan of local history. The loudest protests seemed to come from people who never used their local line.

In keeping with the age, Bridport wanted a railway. But, in a town ringed with hills and some way from an existing line which could be used to plug Bridport into the system, how and where would such a line run? There were many suggestions; some decidedly cranky, none more so than that mooted in 1845 by a private engineer which would run along the coast from Weymouth to Exeter and pass through Bridport. It never got past the issuing of a prospectus. And no wonder; the problems of climbing the Dorset Downs to the east to reach the town pale into insignificance when one considers the terrain to the west. Chideock Hill and Marshwood Vale, ringed by its hills, would mean threading a way through the Vale to Whitchurch Canonicorum and Wootton Fitzpaine and down to Charmouth, or following the route of the proposed 1812 road.

But both eventually run into the great spine of hills that runs from the coast at Charmouth as far as Crewkerne.

The same problems faced the route suggested in 1845 that would link the English and Bristol Channels—an admirable ambition, given that much of the coal for the Lyme Bay towns came from South Wales and that much of it arrived by sail after making the hazardous trip around Land's End. This scheme went under the name of the Bristol and English Channel Connection Railway and was intended to connect 'Stolford [near Bridgwater] in Somerset and Bridport and Lyme Regis and the harbours connected therewith'. There was only one way to get a railway into Bridport: from the Weymouth-Yeovil line at or around Maiden Newton and down through Toller Porcorum and Powerstock into the eastern end of the town. And that was the way they came.

Not without some trouble, however, especially because of the keen rivalry between the Great Western Railway and the London & South Western. The former proposed the Devon & Somerset Railway running between Maiden Newton and Bridport using the broad gauge. But they were opposed by the LSWR, who favoured narrow-gauge railways, and the plan was thrown out by Parliament. In the end, following a packed meeting in November 1854, a local company was formed which proposed a slightly different line from that the GWR had intended to follow and with a broad gauge track. It was not without its opponents, notably the farmers along the route, many of whom feared that their cows would stop giving milk and their chickens stop laying eggs.

The Bridport Railway Bill received the royal assent on 5 May 1855 and the first sod was cut soon afterwards by Joseph Gundry, the chairman of the newly formed Bridport Railway. Nearly two-and-a-half years later, on 12 November 1857, the line was officially opened. Bridport was *en fête*, the day was declared a public holiday and most shops closed. But a sour note was introduced when the first passen-

125 Like the goods on offer on this stall at a Bridport Hospital Fête in 1921, the ladies' hats are simply stunning.

ger train out of the town was late! Not because of leaves or the wrong kind of snow on the line, but because opening day coincided with Yeovil Fair. Whether this was deliberately so is not now known, but far more people than had been expected crowded into the station. It proved too much for stationmaster Daniel Bingham and his staff, who could not issue all the tickets in time. The later-than-scheduled departure meant that the train missed its connection with the 'up' train from Weymouth at Maiden Newton and there was such a long wait for the next train that passengers did not reach Yeovil until midday. There were some complaints, but most Bridport people were delighted with their new railway; especially the tradespeople of the town who now had a quicker route in and out for their goods. One of them was reported in *The Bridport News* as saying that 'it was so smooth that one gentleman had actually written a letter while travelling'.

A round of celebratory dinners followed the opening. First to tuck in were the navvies who had done the actual work. They had a feast of beef and strong beer, the latter so plentiful that many of them confessed to being 'quite glorious' afterwards. A more sumptuous repast followed at the *Bull*, where 140 of the more important people, the local M.P.s, the mayor, the town councillors, the various priests,

representatives of the Great Western Railway Company who had travelled in on the first 'down' train to Bridport (it dared not be late), and the town's business community, spent hours listening to the speeches. *The Bridport News* dealt with the navvies' meal in a few lines, the banquet and its speeches were spread over several columns on two pages. Also disposed of briefly in a few lines were the two private celebratory dinners at the *Cross Keys*, where 52 sat down to Mr. Alderman's food, and a 'large party' at the *Seven Stars* which was run at the time by Mr. Dark.

The new station in St Andrew's Road was originally lit by naphtha lamps although with five trains daily to start with (later reduced to four) after-dark traffic could hardly have been very heavy. John Hallett, a Bridport man, was the first recorded person to be fined for travelling on the line without a ticket. Caught at Maiden Newton in 1883, he was fined 25s. with 22s. costs after the magistrates refused to accept his plea that he had arrived at Bridport station too late to buy a ticket.

There was still talk (from the Lyme Regis end) in 1871 of extending the proposed Lyme Regis branch line from Axminster as far as Bridport and on to West Bay. But, by the time the Lyme branch was finally opened in 1903, that idea had died a natural death.

126 The drill ground at Coniston School, Victoria Grove, 1903. The school was established as a Boarding and Day School for boys in 1889, after having been previously, and for several years, a day school in other premises. It had its own string band.

127 Allington Sunday School on parade around 1910.

128 Laurel House, North Allington (around 1908) is on the left and Allington Infants School can be seen in the background.

129 The circus hits town around 1910.

Otherwise, until the Bridport line was extended to West Bay on 31 March 1884, the only event to disturb the even tenor of life on the line was the conversion from broad to standard gauge in June 1874 which needed the line's closure for a few days.

Pressure to extend the Bridport branch line to the harbour had been growing for some time before the extension was finally opened on 31 March 1884 after taking 12 months to complete. *The Bridport News* cast aside its usual staid manner of reporting and waxed lyrical with:

> Peace hath her victories
> No less renown'd than war.

The town joined with its paper and celebrated the occasion in the usual exuberant Bridport fashion. A rash of bunting and flags appeared, most shops closed and people flocked behind the Volunteers' Band to the new East Street station, which then had an attractive, thatched

DRILL HALL, BRIDPORT.

For ONE NIGHT Only,

SATURDAY, Sept. 16th, 1911.

———————

Percy Tyler & Dudley Stuart's
COMPANY,

In the Sensational Play from the
COMEDY THEATRE, London,

"RAFFLES"

THE AMATEUR CRACKSMAN.

———————

Reserved Seats 3/-;   Second 2/- ;
Admission 1/-,

Doors open 7-30.   Commence at 8.
Early Doors at 7-15.

Seats booked at Messrs. W. Frost's, West Street

130 Saturday night at the Drill Hall was a popular event in Bridport in the first quarter of the century, and tickets sold well at Frost's shop in West Street. 'Raffles' was the attraction on 16 September 1911 and the cost of admission was either a shilling, two shillings or three shillings.

station house, pulled down when the station was rebuilt in 1904. The 14-coach train that arrived from Maiden Newton needed two engines to pull it to West Bay where a public luncheon was held. The children were not forgotten, 1,100 of them marching to the station school by school, the order in which the schools marched being decided by drawing lots. Each pupil received an orange and a bun, what was left over being distributed among the workhouse inmates. The children did not alight when their train reached West Bay because it was not thought wise to let them loose unattended, and, after a short stop, the train took them back to the East Street station. Unsurprisingly, the extra police drafted in from neighbouring towns reported an orderly day with no arrests or incidents apart from a horse and cart falling into the harbour basin. Both were rescued unharmed. The children's ban also meant that the sports organised at West Bay that day was an adult-only affair.

The only jarring note came from the weather, desultory rain doing its best to dampen both the people and (unsuccessfully) their spirits. A triumphal arch of greenery and flags built near East Street station declared 'Success to the Railway' and 'Prosperity to West Bay', neither of which ever really happened.

The line to the town, if not on to West Bay, would outlive Beeching, even if it was one of his prime targets for closure in 1966. The harbour extension went early, the rails coming up in 1965 but, despite its being due for closure on 3 October 1966, the line from Bridport to Maiden Newton survived until 3 May 1975, when the last train departed from the town. Final closure of the Bridport branch line would, said British Rail, save £54,000. Whatever the savings, any later thoughts of re-opening the line were firmly scotched when Barrack Street was closed at its junction with East Street and the Beaminster road continued into Bridport from St Andrew's Road and the old station, along a new road built on the old rail bed. It was named Sea Road North. Later the eastern end of the Bridport link road also followed the rail track as far as the point where it crossed West Bay Road. Not unnaturally, if with considerable lack of imagination, this stretch became Sea Road South.

The line had its moments, especially early in its life when the first Easter Monday train to travel the line brought 200 passengers from Bath, 200 from Bristol, and there were 400 tickets sold to locals at East Street station, good going, especially as West Bay did not have any special attractions laid on. A few weeks later, on Whit Monday, 1,000 tickets for West Bay were issued at East Street but, when the 15.38 train arrived, it only had six coaches, all of them nearly full with trippers from Maiden Newton and stations beyond. The train went to West Bay and came straight back to East Street. It was even worse that evening when everyone seemed to want to catch the seven o'clock train home. Those that did not had to wait until nine, when the train went as far as

East Street and then back to West Bay before finally making its belated way to Maiden Newton. The Bridport Railway Company promised a better service in future.

Part of that service was a cheap return ticket on the 'Bather's Special'. One bought a threepenny ticket and caught the seven o'clock morning train from the main station or the 7.03 from East Street where the ticket was only tuppence-ha'peny. After enjoying a dip, one could make the return journey either on the 7.45 or the 10.10 train from West Bay that same morning. Despite the railway extension there was still enough trade to enable the *Greyhound Hotel* to continue its regular horse bus service to the sea. Perhaps regular is not the best word to use. The journey cost the same as by rail, three pence, but if there were sufficient demand at West Bay for the bus to make an extra trip to, say, Burton Bradstock, that demand would be met and people hoping for a ride back into town would have to wait

or walk. The *Greyhound*'s bus would become motorised in time, and, perhaps with a just a hint of *sic transit gloria mundi* about it, ended its life as a fish and chip van.

A one-horse bus service that served Bridport regularly was run by Warren's from Lyme Regis. It left Lyme daily and reached Bridport in time for the passengers to catch the midday train to Maiden Newton. The return journey to Lyme Regis was not made until the late afternoon train had arrived. The last Warren's coach ran in 1924, when it gave up the unequal struggle with the buses and charabancs that began to appear in Bridport soon after the First World War.

The Royal Mail carried passengers as well but would not accept liability for any article of luggage lost or damaged exceeding the value of £5 unless it had been entered as such on boarding and been paid for accordingly.

The horseless carriage reached West Dorset around the turn of the century, and the posting

131 West Street around 1905, from a W. & E. Frost postcard. William Frost's is the shop on the left with a man standing outside the window. It was from a room at the rear in 1855 that he first published *The Bridport News*, which was produced there until 1962 when the publication passed out of the Frost family's hands.

houses, inns and stables which had endured a 50-year slump because of the coming of the railway, had new life breathed into them, although for many years the horse remained king on the Bridport streets. Some of the men who used the hotels were company representatives. Formerly they had arrived at a town by train and hired a carriage if they had to make country calls, but after the First World War the motor car made them increasingly mobile. The *Bull* was a favourite Bridport haunt for travellers, not least because it hired out horse-drawn carriages and also met every train that arrived with its own horse-drawn, later motor-ised, omnibus. It also stabled the horses for the local fire engine and, for many years, the black plumes so popular with Victorian undertakers for their funeral horses were stored there.

The St Andrew's Road-based engineering firm of E.A. Chard & Company dabbled with the manufacture of motor-car engines. It was a short-lived dabbling, but one of their BRIT engines is said to be buried on the outskirts of Beaminster in the former premises of John Hunt's Steam Sawmills and Carriage Accessories. Hunt used a replacement engine and gearbox in a modified Daimler to give penny rides around the town. Not unnaturally it was known as the 'Beaminster Bus'. A few other cars were made and mostly sold locally. The Beaminster Bus was registered in 1904 and had an FX94 number; Dorset numbers originally bore the prefix BF but, for obvious reasons, there was an outcry and the numbers were changed to FX.

In 1903 George Bonfield changed his business in East Street from that of a sanitary engineer and cycle repairer into a garage. A few years later he moved to the foot of West Street where the business is still in his family's hands.

George Bonfield ran charabancs from his West Street garage, a trip to Gough's Cave being particularly popular for club and church outings. But, with early charabancs restricted to a 12 m.p.h. speed limit and fitted with solid tyres until around the mid-1920s when pneu-matic tyres began to appear, it must have been a long, hard journey. Later, the Bluebird Company covered the Dorset coast as far as Bournemouth with their charabancs. They operated from a depot in West Street where the Somerfield supermarket now stands.

Hackney carriages appeared in the town in the early 20th century and provision was made for parking them at different spots, including, silly as it seems now, three spaces in front of the Town Hall; they were not to go any closer than six feet from the corner of South Street. Others were on the west side of South Street, by the market and also the pig market.

Because of its position on the main Folkestone-Exeter trunk route, traffic jams and Bridport had become synonymous long before work began on the £1,800,000 link road which was opened three weeks ahead of schedule in July 1988, 50 years after the first talk of the need for a bypass. Performing the ceremony, Roads Minister Peter Bottomley declared that it would mean 'many less [sic] accidents, many less [sic] injuries and much less misery'. Two hours later the first accident on the new road occurred.

It had not been thought fit for the Bridport Chamber of Commerce to be at the opening ceremony, which its secretary Ron Brickwood claimed was 'an insult', and with some justification. The Chamber, along with many others, thought that the road markings at the Miles Cross junction at the western end of the new road were dangerous. They had a point: there were as many as 11 accidents at the spot within three weeks of opening day, but the Ministry declared it was perfectly safe—and then promptly changed the road markings.

Today Bridport's South, East and West Streets look just as crowded, albeit with more cars and fewer lorries, as they did before the bypass was built. Happily for the town's commercial life there are adequate parking facilities, and the West Dorset equivalent of 'the world and his wife' still come to the town to shop.

Chapter Seven

The First World War

Erected in proud and grateful memory of the men
of Bridport who fell in the war of 1914-1918.
Their name liveth for Evermore.

Bridport War Memorial, Thursday, May 27th, 1920

Bridport learnt that Britain was at war with Germany on 4 August 1914 from the offices of *The Bridport News* in West Street, where the window became a focal point for townspeople anxious for news of the fighting in Belgium and France. The newspaper told the town that it had arranged to receive war telegrams from the Press Association in London and they would be on sale in printed form at one halfpenny per copy. The *News* also stated that 'nowhere in the country is the patriotic spirit more marked, now that the perils of war have burst upon the country, than in Bridport, whose loyalty has ever been unswerving to the Crown and Empire'. No doubt similar sentiments were being expressed in other local newspapers throughout the country.

Paper shortages forced the *News* to reduce itself by half to four pages although its price stayed at one penny. To be fair, its advertising revenue was also reduced. It did bring out eight-page papers again on the odd occasion but, until after the Armistice, four pages became the norm. But it was too late to interfere with or block an advertisement in its first wartime edition which warned readers to 'Be Prepared'. It had nothing to do with the war, Messrs.

F.W. & E.R. Best were advising their customers to take one of their 17s. 6d. or 22s. 6d. waterproofs with them on holiday.

All the banks remained closed owing to an extension of the Bank Holiday, and other early casualties in Bridport included the West Bay Regatta and Messrs. Cousens's steamer trips which would no longer ply between the harbour and other neighbouring seaside towns. The regatta had first been held in 1844 and had become one of the highlights of the Bridport year (although it was only staged once in a 19-year spell that began in 1876). In the interests of security, and to help the censors, all telegrams for overseas addresses handed in at Bridport Post Office had to be written in English (French was acceptable for Switzerland).

But, despite the strident claims of *The Bridport News* and the nationally held view that the war would be over by Christmas, there was much unpatriotic stockpiling of groceries in anticipation of a long and hungry war.

The Dorset Territorial Battalion RFA had an impressive send-off from a packed station. Left behind to take over, Bridport Boy Scout Troop took up the guarding of the town's water supplies in the reservoir at the

Bothenhampton Quarries when, with the paranoia that is much in evidence at such times, the authorities decided that German spies might poison the country's drinking water. Almost as bad was the arrest of Mr. James Rennie for spying on Eggardon Hill. Rennie, a Londoner staying at Weymouth, was reported to be taking notes there in 'a suspicious manner'. He was released when it became apparent that he was an archaeologist studying in the area.

On Sunday 9 August, Bridport held an Intercession Service at St Mary's for divine mercy and the safety of the nation and empire. Although memories would not have stretched back to 1588, when the coasts of England were lined with beacons which were lit when news reached Plymouth that the Armada had been seen off the Lizard, the same method of warning

of possible German invaders was put into use, and Lieutenant-Colonel Colfox erected a beacon on West Bay's East Cliff along with others at Thorncombe Beacon and near Abbotsbury. No one thought to ask how the German fleet were going to force a passage through the Straits of Dover, or to suggest that East Anglia would have been the obvious landing place for an invader from Germany.

There was expectation of heavy casualties and Bridport, like so many other small towns, had been prepared for this by the formation of a Voluntary Aid Detachment (VAD) of the Red Cross Society. Miss C. Colfox had been a prime mover in its formation some time before the war and she immediately placed its services at the disposal of the authorities.

132 & 133 Many a Bridport window sported a card to show that a husband or son was 'serving his King, Country and Empire'. Lt. Robert Spencer was one such husband.

134   1st Battalion, Dorset Regiment, in camp opposite Bridport station in August 1910.

Bridport women helped in other (unexpected) ways as well. Miss Fenwick, the secretary of the West Dorset Suffrage Movement, wrote to the mayor to say they would no longer be indulging in politics and that her movement placed its services at his disposal.

Bridport's Ambulance Association put itself on a war footing, forming into parties of stretcher-bearers ready to move wounded soldiers from East Street station to the hospital. The Secondary School was requisitioned as a hospital but, when the summer holidays ended a few days later, it was taken back by the education authorities. No doubt there was disappointment throughout the town when Bridport was told it would not be used for military hospital purposes. It was, it seems, only able to accommodate half a train-load of wounded troops at the station, and that did not make economic sense.

But Bridport helped in other ways, besides sending its sons to fight on every front. Its ladies buckled down to knitting comforts for the troops and a Bridport working party was formed on 14 September 1914 to channel these efforts in the right direction. By the end of the war the working party had sent around 8,000 articles to the forces, including over 2,000 shirts and some 1,300 pairs of socks, as well as pyjamas, bed-socks, towels and other items. Food parcels were sent regularly, particularly to Bridport men who had become prisoners-of-war. Another valuable source of local help was the Bridport War Hospital Supply Depot formed by Mrs. C. Sanctuary in 1917, which met in South Street to make surgical dressings for neighbouring hospitals. By the end of the war they had despatched over 13,000 of them. Sphagnum moss was in demand as a dressing for wounds and the job of collecting and taking

135 The 1st Battalion, Dorset Regiment, turning right into East Street on 4 August 1910 on their way to a now-unknown destination. They had been camping opposite Bridport station and, appropriately, are seen here leaving Barrack Street.

136 The Bridport and Beaminster 'Bhoys' of A Company, 2/4 Dorsets in camp at Ahmednagar, India, in 1915.

137 West Dorset men, including some from Bridport, at Codford Camp in June 1916 shortly before leaving for France.

it to the railway station for despatch to military hospitals was given to the 1st Bridport Scout Troop.

Bridport lost most of its horses overnight. Apart from those granted exemption on essential grounds, those which belonged to doctors and farmers for example, they were all commandeered by the military authorities. Bridport's equine conscripts were marshalled at a collecting point in St Michael's Lane. But the town's main ingredients for the war machine were men and rope, and Bridport was represented wherever Britain fought, especially on the high seas, as was only to be expected of a West Country port. The names of all the 150 local men who died in action or from wounds or illness during the First World War can be found on the war memorial outside St Mary's Church, including that of Albert Greenham, thought to be Bridport's first victim of the war, who was lost with HMS *Hawke* when she was torpedoed in the North Sea on 15 October 1914. It became the custom to read out the names of the latest fatalities at the Wednesday evening church service.

It is said that few recruiting officers excelled as the Rector of Bridport, Canon H.R.W. Farrer, when it came to exhorting local men to join up and fight for their country. He claimed that:

> It is not the time for young men to remain sitting upon their stools in the banks or the counting houses. Every young man must decide, either to his shame to stay at home, or he must answer his country's call now.

It was ever thus; the loudest cries to young men to go and die coming from older men and women who would not be going or dying. Such older men included one local newspaper editor who, self-righteously, wrote that the *Pulman's Weekly News* would not be covering any football or cricket matches that might be played. 'Young men would be better employed at the front'; but his paper gave its usual coverage to fox-hunting. (Perhaps fox-hunting

is not sport?) To be fair to Canon Farrer, Rector of Bridport between 1895 and 1916, his son, Major Farrer, went out to France in August 1914 and, after being wounded six times and winning the Military Cross and two bars and the Belgian Croix-de-Guerre, was killed right at the end of the war on 30 October 1918. There is a memorial to him in his father's church.

The Bridport News listed the names of the men of the town who had already joined up. There were 125 such names within three weeks and ever-increasing lists were published at regular intervals. But, all too soon and all too often, *The Bridport News* was also publishing obituaries of the men killed in action. The men and women left behind were recommended to learn to shoot by Mr. J. Sutill, the secretary of Bridport Rifle Club.

A committee had been quickly formed in August 1914 to meet the needs of the unemployed. But it is an ill wind that blows nobody any good and, although one of Bridport's main markets for nets, the fishing trade in the North and Baltic seas, was lost, orders poured in from the government for military purposes and full employment was guaranteed.

If it was made from rope, Bridport could supply it. And it is surprising into how many remote corners of the army or navy machine Bridport sent its products. Nets to hold vegetables when they were being boiled in giant tuns by front-line kitchens; made in Bridport. Camouflage netting; made in Bridport. Tent-lines and hammocks; made in Bridport. Sailors' lanyards and whipcord safety-pin rings for hand-grenades; made in Bridport. Rifle pull-through cords and hay nets for horses; made in Bridport. Battleships flew their ensigns and signal flags on ropes made in Bridport.

The anti-Hun paranoia that swept a normally sane country, and led to a British King changing his family name and the sacking of a First Lord of the Admiralty who was German, also led to the stoning of shop

138 *Left.* Unveiling the war memorial.

139 *Below.* An Armistice Day service around 1930.

140 *Right.* The memorial to Major Henry Farrer, M.C. and 2 bars and Croix-de-Guerre, at St Mary's. He was the son of Canon Farrer, Rector of Bridport between 1895-1916.

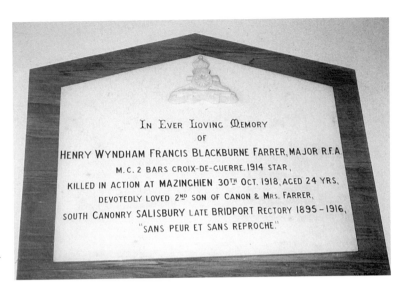

IN EVER LOVING MEMORY
OF
HENRY WYNDHAM FRANCIS BLACKBURNE FARRER, MAJOR R.F.A.
M.C. 2 BARS CROIX-DE-GUERRE. 1914 STAR,
KILLED IN ACTION AT MAZINGHIEN 30TH OCT. 1918, AGED 24 YRS,
DEVOTEDLY LOVED 2ND SON OF CANON & MRS. FARRER,
SOUTH CANONRY SALISBURY LATE BRIDPORT RECTORY 1895-1916,
"SANS PEUR ET SANS REPROCHE."

windows whose owners had Germanic names and, worst of all, from a nation of so-called animal-lovers, to the physical abuse of dachshunds (Alsatians were too big for the cowards). This paranoia reached Bridport when the *King of Prussia Inn* (with a double dose of patriotism) changed its name to the *King of the Belgians*. In the Second World War, as befitted a town that had roped his fleet, it changed again, this time to the *Lord Nelson*. The Germans nearly had their revenge in the Second World War, just missing the inn with a bomb.

When the town was asked by the National Committee to purchase £15,000 of war bonds, the equivalent of six aeroplanes, it staged a Business Men's Week between 4-9 August 1918. Bridport Aeroplane Bank was set up at 26 East Street and run by the postmaster and the managers of all the local banks. No less than £69,070 was raised but, with the end of the fighting less than three months away, it is doubtful whether any 'Bridport' aeroplane reached the front.

The news that the Armistice had been signed at five o'clock on the morning of 11 November and that it would become effective at eleven o'clock, reached the Royal Naval Airship Station at Powerstock at 6.30 p.m., the news being telephoned to Bridport and announced by the Mayor, and also posted in the window at the West Street office of *The Bridport News* soon afterwards. Almost immediately, all business premises and shops shut their doors, and the town half-vanished under a sea of bunting and flags. Motor cars, horses, even some dogs, sported red, white and blue favours as well as the colours of all the Allies. And, as the guns in Flanders fell silent for the first time in over four years, the Town Hall clock, silent for those same four long years, struck the 11th hour. Half an hour later, with the echoes of the old bells at St Mary's Church still winging their way across the town, a packed congregation, along with the hundreds left outside, opened a Thanksgiving Service with the old 100th, *All People That On Earth Do Dwell*. Later that day hundreds of people attended an open-air meeting outside the Town Hall, at which the Mayor, was the main speaker.

Bridport's war memorial was unveiled on 27 May 1920 by Lieutenant-Colonel T.A. Colfox, High Sheriff of Dorset. Designed by Sir Gilbert Scott, A.R.A., F.R.I.B.A., the architect of Liverpool Cathedral, its column and base wall are of Doulting stone, the panels on which the names of the fallen are recorded are, appropriately, of more local Portland stone. It cost around £750, the money being raised by public subscription. South Street, closed to traffic for the occasion, was crowded with over 3,000 people including the curate, Canon J.W. Coulter, Rev. A.S. Martin of the Baptist Church, Rev. H. Webb (Congregationalist), and T.P.N. Field and T. Taylor (both from the Methodist Church).

Chapter Eight

The Second World War

His Majesty visited a well-known seaside resort whose civil population became aware and hundreds collected in the main street to watch him and his aides depart after they had partaken of tea served in a hostelry.

The Bridport News, September 1939

Unlike 1914, by the time the German armies spilled across the Polish frontier on 1 September 1939, most people had long been convinced that another war was inevitable and preparations for the evacuation of children from areas at serious risk of intense air attack and for the introduction of trained ARP (Air Raid Precautions) personnel were virtually complete.

The local branch of Woolworth had already staged a practice evacuation of its premises and announced, with due pride, that

it had been done in three minutes. The evacuees began arriving at Bridport station a day or so after Britain's entry into the war, 800 of them to be billeted in the town, the other 600 in the neighbouring villages. They were mostly children between the ages of three and 14, but there were some mothers among them. Most were from the Senior Street School in Paddington, whose entire 136-strong Infants Class had made the journey; all were met by the senior pupils of Bridport Grammar School who acted as marshals and took them to the

141 George VI leaves the *Bull* after having tea there in September 1939.

121

142 Bridport ATC (Air Training Corp) Squadron entering South Street when parading through the town around 1943-4.

143 Bridport's Mayor, Councillor Henry Hounsell, inspecting a naval detachment at a military parade in 1940 in Dorset, but not in Bridport.

school which was to be used as a distribution centre. From there they were taken by car or bus to their final destinations. Many of the children had 'clothes showing signs of poverty' and, to add to what had to be a traumatic and tearful occasion, it was raining.

Given the circumstances, the arrival and distribution proceedings passed without any real hitches, although one woman with two children flatly refused to stay and eventually got a lift home in a furniture van that was going to London. There were seven Cypriot Greeks, only one of whom could speak English (and was hardly likely to be able to do so with a slow, West-Country drawl), and two young Swiss ladies whose schoolgirl English was limited.

They came to a Bridport already blacked out at night, although cars parked in South Street now had to leave their side lights switched on. They came to a town whose ARP Report Centre's manning level was completed

by the time night fell on the first day of the war. They came to a town that had started distributing its respirators on 30 August and had completed it on the morning that a sad, tired-sounding Neville Chamberlain told Bridport that it was at war with Germany. Seven local couples, fearful of an uncertain future, rushed off to John Roper, the local Registrar, and applied for special marriage licences.

In that first month of the war, King George VI visited troops in the West Country but, with spies said to be everywhere, even *The Bridport News* was only allowed to report that His Majesty 'visited a well-known seaside resort whose civil population became aware and hundreds collected in the main street to watch him and his aides depart after they had partaken of tea served in a hostelry'. In other words, he had stopped at the *Bull* in Bridport.

The war began to bite. The announcement that petrol was to be rationed saw a last-minute rush to fill up at local filling stations. There was a seven-day reprieve and the last-minute rush took place all over again a week later. Shops again reported heavy sales in food, especially of the tinned variety, as the good people of Bridport prepared for a long war.

The fall of France and the threat of invasion led to the national call for recruits for the Local Defence Volunteers (LDV) which was quickly renamed the Home Guard. 'Dad's Army' served Bridport well until its stand-down at the end of 1944, meeting at the British Legion Hall in Victoria Grove. Members held their shooting practices at a range at Colmers Hill near Symondsbury.

When a rumour swept the area that the Germans had landed near Poole, a Home Guard road block was set up at Bradpole. The first man to be challenged by the indomitable Dad's Army with a cry of 'Halt, who goes there?' received the reply 'You ***** well know, you see me every day.'

At Seatown the Home Guard were the proud possessors of a six-pound gun which, although dug in, camouflage-netted and intended for firing at seaborne invaders, seemed more often than not to be pointing at the windows of the *Anchor*. Happily, for both the seaborne invaders and the landlord of the *Anchor*, the gun was never fired, even in practice. But a cow did wander into a nearby, wired-off minefield via the river and, after several policemen and soldiers arrived and spent some time puzzling how best to get it out, it wandered out the same way on its own account. The BBC's *Dad's Army* has nothing on Seatown.

During 1940 the proceedings of Bridport's 'War Weapons Week', one of many savings drives staged throughout the country, raised just over £200,000. The money went towards the building of HMS *Bridport*, a coastal patrol boat. After the war it was taken over by the RAF, became HMAFV *Bridport*, and was used in air-sea rescue work. Later still, after decommissioning in 1958, the ship's bell, originally a gift from the town, ended up in Bridport Town Hall. 'Salute the Soldier Week' raised £120,000 for which the town received a plaque.

Bridport was good at raising money—and other things as well. With shipping space at a premium many commodities were salvaged and recycled. Householders were asked to hand over waste paper, old books and newsprint. Often old and large family Bibles were sacrificed, destroying many families' recorded histories. Most railings vanished, including those around churchyards, and old bedsteads joined them in the melting pot. Aluminium saucepans and other utensils went towards the manufacture of aeroplanes. Salvage was collected right through the war and beyond, and a week after VE Day the Town Council were told that the latest quarterly return showed that £76 had gone into the town's coffers through the sale of salvage. Included in that was nine tons of waste paper, six tons of baled tins, six hundredweight of bones, and 163 jam jars which were sold at 5s. 6d. per dozen. Vital

144 This photograph of the first HMS *Bridport* was presented to the Borough of Bridport by the captain, officers and men of the vessel in appreciation of the town's generosity. It was taken on 17 May 1941 and now hangs in the Town Hall.

145 The second HMS *Bridport* was commissioned on 6 November 1993. Its picture also hangs in the Town Hall.

146 *Right.* At the end of the Second World War, the first HMS *Bridport* was taken over by the RAF and used as an air-sea rescue launch. The ship's bell was presented to Squadron Leader E.W. Hardie, the commanding officer, by Mayor Mr. J. Dale. Mr. Dale served from 1940 until the end of the war.

147 *Below right.* The bell of HMS *Bridport* beneath the Borough's shield.

cash was raised for financing the war effort through the sale of National Savings stamps at school and by volunteers calling weekly and on a house-to-house basis to sell the stamps along with Savings Certificates and War Bonds.

Bridport's knitting needles were soon in action again making 'comforts' for the troops. Volunteers were issued with wool and patterns, mostly for socks, mittens, jumpers and scarves. At Bridport Grammar School, when one master joined the Army, senior girls were asked to knit articles to send him along with letters telling of life at the school. Fifty years later, at a school reunion, he produced the letters that he kept all those years.

Life at the school was often interrupted by the air-raid warning. Then pupils went to specially-dug trenches under the hedges at the top of the sports field which had galvanised roofs to keep them all dry. In the shelters the children wore coats, dyed to look like camouflage, which parents had been asked to provide for their children. Many a Sunday-best coat ended its days in this fashion. Senior girls were introduced to the delights of ring doughnuts and peanut butter when they volunteered to serve food to the American soldiers who used the canteen the Red Cross had opened on the first floor at the Literary and Scientific Institute in East Street.

The Luftwaffe did visit Bridport. A house that once stood on what is now the entrance to the East Street car park was destroyed on a December market day when the *Lord Nelson*,

148   American soldiers enjoy tea and cakes at the American Red Cross Club in the Literary and Scientific Institute in East Street in August 1944.

just two doors away, was crowded. In between the wrecked house and the *Lord Nelson* was George Elliott's grocery shop. It was badly damaged but, with the aid of several wooden props to keep a sagging ceiling from caving in, the debris was cleared and George, who had managed to stockpile some Christmas goodies for his regulars, 'opened as usual' and made sure they all had a reasonably Happy Christmas.

Damage was also suffered by quite a few neighbouring buildings, including the General Infants School just behind, which had many of its windows blown out, the children being showered by glass and dust. Another such raid saw a bomb destroy property and cause loss of life just behind the *Star* in West Street; Mrs. Alice Cast was killed as she was posting a letter to her son in the Navy. Luckier was George Hecks. The blast went through a passage at the side of the *Star* and blew him across the street. One bomb that hit the Westminster Bank failed

to explode, although it took some days to dig it out and traffic had to be diverted through Rax Lane. Four bombs landed in the field opposite the Broadmead council estate at Chideock which, oddly enough, was originally going to be built in that same field around the time of the First World War.

The V-bomb attacks on south-east England in 1944 caused considerable damage, and Bridport's WI, with the aid of the Boy Scouts, collected a mountain of gifts for the people of a 'shattered Woolwich'.

Rationing hit the town, but country communities such as Bridport were not so badly situated as large towns and cities. There was a reasonable supply of milk and eggs at neighbouring farms, rabbits were always plentiful in the countryside, and many households also reared them in their gardens. And there were always nuts, blackberries and mushrooms when in season.

Peace, when it came, was celebrated in Bridport's own fashion, with bunting, flags, bells and the band, and street parties at which, despite the shortages through rationing, vast quantities of sandwiches and cakes vanished. The children were also treated to a celebratory tea, 1,200 being given tea and ices in the two drill halls and later a free cinema show at the Palace; how many sittings were required for the entire 1,200 is not now known. Even the licensing authorities, not known to favour the frivolous, unbent to the extent of allowing an hour's extension on VE Day itself. That fact is said to have no connection with the action of the Town Council who postponed for a week its meeting due on the evening of VE Day.

There were still 230 evacuees in the town at the end of the war. Those who made their own way home had to pay their own train fares. Not all wanted to return; the country way of life appealed so much that a few families stayed on—for good.

VJ Day, when it arrived, was not celebrated with quite the fervour of VE Day. But celebrated it was. Crowds gathered and street dancing continued until the late hours after a Thanksgiving service had been held.

Bridport may not have had to 'fight 'em on the beaches and the landing grounds', but even Winston Churchill would have admitted that the town had 'Done its Bit'.

149   Market day in West Street on 29 January 1913.

Bibliography

Dorset Federation of Women's Institutes, *Dorset Within Living Memory* (1990)

Gutteridge, Roger, *Dorset Smugglers* (1984)

Harper, Charles, *The Dorset Coast* (1905)

Houghton, George, *Bridport and West Dorset Golf Club* (1991)

Hutchins, John, *The History and Antiquities of the County of Dorset* (1774)

Jackson, B.L. and Tattershall, M.J., *The Bridport Branch* (1976)

Maskell, Joseph, *The History of the Topography of Bridport* (1855)

Penn, K.J., *Historical Towns in Dorset* (1980)

Ricketts, Elizabeth, *The Almshouses of Dorset* (1970)

Rowson, J.W., *Bridport and The Great War* (1923)

Symonds, Henry, *Bridport Harbour Through Seven Centuries* (1931)

Weinstock, M.B, *Old Dorset* (1967)

Whitehouse, John, *St Mary's Parish Church* (1989; available at the church)

Young, Jimmy, *Old Dorset Brewers* (1985)

Index